Risk Committee
Complete Self-Assessment Gu

C000155294

The guidance in this Self-Assessment i
practices and standards in business pr
quality management. The guidance is also based on the professional
judgment of the individual collaborators listed in the Acknowledgments.

Notice of rights

Trademarks

Table of Contents

About The Art of Service

The Art of Service, Business Process Architects since 2000, is dedicated to helping stakeholders achieve excellence.

Defining, designing, creating, and implementing a process to solve a stakeholders challenge or meet an objective is the most valuable role… In EVERY group, company, organization and department.

Unless you're talking a one-time, single-use project, there should be a process. Whether that process is managed and implemented by humans, AI, or a combination of the two, it needs to be designed by someone with a complex enough perspective to ask the right questions.

Someone capable of asking the right questions and step back and say, 'What are we really trying to accomplish here? And is there a different way to look at it?'

With The Art of Service's Standard Requirements Self-Assessments, we empower people who can do just that — whether their title is marketer, entrepreneur, manager, salesperson, consultant, Business Process Manager, executive assistant, IT Manager, CIO etc... —they are the people who rule the future. They are people who watch the process as it happens, and ask the right questions to make the process work better.

Contact us when you need any support with this Self-Assessment and any help with templates, blue-prints and examples of standard documents you might need:

http://theartofservice.com
service@theartofservice.com

Included Resources - how to access

Included with your purchase of the book is the Risk Committee

Self-Assessment Spreadsheet Dashboard which contains all questions and Self-Assessment areas and auto-generates insights, graphs, and project RACI planning - all with examples to get you started right away.

How? Simply send an email to
access@theartofservice.com
with this books' title in the subject to get the Risk Committee Self Assessment Tool right away.

You will receive the following contents with New and Updated specific criteria:

• The latest quick edition of the book in PDF

• The latest complete edition of the book in PDF, which criteria correspond to the criteria in...

• The Self-Assessment Excel Dashboard, and...

• Example pre-filled Self-Assessment Excel Dashboard to get familiar with results generation

• In-depth specific Checklists covering the topic

• Project management checklists and templates to assist with implementation

INCLUDES LIFETIME SELF ASSESSMENT UPDATES

Every self assessment comes with Lifetime Updates and Lifetime Free Updated Books. Lifetime Updates is an industry-first feature which allows you to receive verified self assessment updates, ensuring you always have the most accurate information at your fingertips.

Get it now- you will be glad you did - do it now, before you forget.

Send an email to **access@theartofservice.com** with this books' title in the subject to get the Risk Committee Self Assessment Tool right away.

Purpose of this Self-Assessment

This Self-Assessment has been developed to improve understanding of the requirements and elements of Risk Committee, based on best practices and standards in business process architecture, design and quality management.

It is designed to allow for a rapid Self-Assessment to determine how closely existing management practices and procedures correspond to the elements of the Self-Assessment.

The criteria of requirements and elements of Risk Committee have been rephrased in the format of a Self-Assessment questionnaire, with a seven-criterion scoring system, as explained in this document.

In this format, even with limited background knowledge of Risk Committee, a manager can quickly review existing operations to determine how they measure up to the standards. This in turn can serve as the starting point of a 'gap analysis' to identify management tools or system elements that might usefully be implemented in the organization to help improve overall performance.

How to use the Self-Assessment

On the following pages are a series of questions to identify to what extent your Risk Committee initiative is complete in comparison to the requirements set in standards.

To facilitate answering the questions, there is a space in front of each question to enter a score on a scale of '1' to '5'.

1 Strongly Disagree

2 Disagree

3 Neutral

4 Agree

5 Strongly Agree

Read the question and rate it with the following in front of mind:

'In my belief, the answer to this question is clearly defined'.

There are two ways in which you can choose to interpret this statement;
1. how aware are you that the answer to the question is clearly defined
2. for more in-depth analysis you can choose to gather evidence and confirm the answer to the question. This obviously will take more time, most Self-Assessment users opt for the first way to interpret the question and dig deeper later on based on the outcome of the overall Self-Assessment.

A score of '1' would mean that the answer is not clear at all, where a '5' would mean the answer is crystal clear and defined. Leave emtpy when the question is not applicable or you don't want to answer it, you can skip it without affecting your score. Write your score in the space provided.

After you have responded to all the appropriate statements in each section, compute your average score for that section, using the formula provided, and round to the nearest tenth. Then transfer to the corresponding spoke in the Risk Committee Scorecard on the second next page of the Self-Assessment.

Your completed Risk Committee Scorecard will give you a clear presentation of which Risk Committee areas need attention.

Risk Committee Scorecard Example

Example of how the finalized Scorecard can look like:

Risk Committee Scorecard

Your Scores:

BEGINNING OF THE SELF-ASSESSMENT:

CRITERION #1: RECOGNIZE

INTENT: Be aware of the need for change. Recognize that there is an unfavorable variation, problem or symptom.

In my belief, the answer to this question is clearly defined:

5 Strongly Agree

4 Agree

3 Neutral

2 Disagree

1 Strongly Disagree

1. How are the Risk Committee's objectives aligned to the group's overall stakeholder strategy?
<--- Score

2. What tools and technologies are needed for a custom Risk Committee project?
<--- Score

3. What is the problem or issue?

<--- Score

4. What are the Risk Committee resources needed?
<--- Score

5. Do you need to avoid or amend any Risk Committee activities?
<--- Score

6. What extra resources will you need?
<--- Score

7. Do you have/need 24-hour access to key personnel?
<--- Score

8. What resources or support might you need?
<--- Score

9. Who needs what information?
<--- Score

10. Are there Risk Committee problems defined?
<--- Score

11. What do employees need in the short term?
<--- Score

12. How do you recognize an objection?
<--- Score

13. What is the extent or complexity of the Risk Committee problem?
<--- Score

14. Why the need?
<--- Score

15. What else needs to be measured?
<--- Score

16. How do you take a forward-looking perspective in identifying Risk Committee research related to market response and models?
<--- Score

17. Is it clear when you think of the day ahead of you what activities and tasks you need to complete?
<--- Score

18. How are training requirements identified?
<--- Score

19. Which issues are too important to ignore?
<--- Score

20. Does the problem have ethical dimensions?
<--- Score

21. What Risk Committee coordination do you need?
<--- Score

22. What are the stakeholder objectives to be achieved with Risk Committee?
<--- Score

23. What training and capacity building actions are needed to implement proposed reforms?
<--- Score

24. Are there regulatory / compliance issues?
<--- Score

25. Why is this needed?
<--- Score

26. Will a response program recognize when a crisis occurs and provide some level of response?
<--- Score

27. Are employees recognized or rewarded for performance that demonstrates the highest levels of integrity?
<--- Score

28. What needs to stay?
<--- Score

29. What vendors make products that address the Risk Committee needs?
<--- Score

30. Who defines the rules in relation to any given issue?
<--- Score

31. Which information does the Risk Committee business case need to include?
<--- Score

32. Does Risk Committee create potential expectations in other areas that need to be recognized and considered?
<--- Score

33. Where do you need to exercise leadership?
<--- Score

34. Who should resolve the Risk Committee issues?

<--- Score

35. To what extent does each concerned units management team recognize Risk Committee as an effective investment?
<--- Score

36. What is the smallest subset of the problem you can usefully solve?
<--- Score

37. What is the problem and/or vulnerability?
<--- Score

38. What information do users need?
<--- Score

39. What Risk Committee events should you attend?
<--- Score

40. Is it needed?
<--- Score

41. How many trainings, in total, are needed?
<--- Score

42. Are employees recognized for desired behaviors?
<--- Score

43. Looking at each person individually – does every one have the qualities which are needed to work in this group?
<--- Score

44. Does your organization need more Risk Committee education?

<--- Score

45. What are the timeframes required to resolve each of the issues/problems?
<--- Score

46. How are you going to measure success?
<--- Score

47. Consider your own Risk Committee project, what types of organizational problems do you think might be causing or affecting your problem, based on the work done so far?
<--- Score

48. Which needs are not included or involved?
<--- Score

49. When a Risk Committee manager recognizes a problem, what options are available?
<--- Score

50. Are controls defined to recognize and contain problems?
<--- Score

51. What are the clients issues and concerns?
<--- Score

52. What are the minority interests and what amount of minority interests can be recognized?
<--- Score

53. How does it fit into your organizational needs and tasks?
<--- Score

54. What situation(s) led to this Risk Committee Self Assessment?
<--- Score

55. Are there any specific expectations or concerns about the Risk Committee team, Risk Committee itself?
<--- Score

56. Are losses recognized in a timely manner?
<--- Score

57. Think about the people you identified for your Risk Committee project and the project responsibilities you would assign to them, what kind of training do you think they would need to perform these responsibilities effectively?
<--- Score

58. Who else hopes to benefit from it?
<--- Score

59. What prevents you from making the changes you know will make you a more effective Risk Committee leader?
<--- Score

60. What needs to be done?
<--- Score

61. What creative shifts do you need to take?
<--- Score

62. How can auditing be a preventative security measure?

<--- Score

63. Will Risk Committee deliverables need to be tested and, if so, by whom?
<--- Score

64. Do you need different information or graphics?
<--- Score

65. What does Risk Committee success mean to the stakeholders?
<--- Score

66. Are you dealing with any of the same issues today as yesterday? What can you do about this?
<--- Score

67. Whom do you really need or want to serve?
<--- Score

68. What Risk Committee capabilities do you need?
<--- Score

69. How much are sponsors, customers, partners, stakeholders involved in Risk Committee? In other words, what are the risks, if Risk Committee does not deliver successfully?
<--- Score

70. Where is training needed?
<--- Score

71. What would happen if Risk Committee weren't done?
<--- Score

72. Are there any revenue recognition issues?
<--- Score

73. Have you identified your Risk Committee key performance indicators?
<--- Score

74. Who are your key stakeholders who need to sign off?
<--- Score

75. For your Risk Committee project, identify and describe the business environment, is there more than one layer to the business environment?
<--- Score

76. What Risk Committee problem should be solved?
<--- Score

77. Who needs to know?
<--- Score

78. What problems are you facing and how do you consider Risk Committee will circumvent those obstacles?
<--- Score

79. Will it solve real problems?
<--- Score

80. What do you need to start doing?
<--- Score

81. Are your goals realistic? Do you need to redefine your problem? Perhaps the problem has changed or maybe you have reached your goal and need to set a

new one?

<--- Score

82. How do you assess your Risk Committee workforce capability and capacity needs, including skills, competencies, and staffing levels?

<--- Score

83. What are the expected benefits of Risk Committee to the stakeholder?

<--- Score

84. How do you identify the kinds of information that you will need?

<--- Score

85. Is the quality assurance team identified?

<--- Score

86. As a sponsor, customer or management, how important is it to meet goals, objectives?

<--- Score

87. What activities does the governance board need to consider?

<--- Score

88. To what extent would your organization benefit from being recognized as a award recipient?

<--- Score

89. Did you miss any major Risk Committee issues?

<--- Score

90. Can management personnel recognize the monetary benefit of Risk Committee?

<--- Score

91. Do you know what you need to know about Risk Committee?
<--- Score

92. Will new equipment/products be required to facilitate Risk Committee delivery, for example is new software needed?
<--- Score

93. Do you recognize Risk Committee achievements?
<--- Score

94. What should be considered when identifying available resources, constraints, and deadlines?
<--- Score

95. What is the Risk Committee problem definition? What do you need to resolve?
<--- Score

96. Would you recognize a threat from the inside?
<--- Score

97. What is the recognized need?
<--- Score

98. Is the need for organizational change recognized?
<--- Score

99. Who needs to know about Risk Committee?
<--- Score

100. What are your needs in relation to Risk Committee skills, labor, equipment, and markets?

<--- Score

Add up total points for this section:
_ _ _ _ _ = Total points for this section

Divided by: _ _ _ _ _ _ (number of
statements answered) = _ _ _ _ _ _
Average score for this section

Transfer your score to the Risk
Committee Index at the beginning of the
Self-Assessment.

CRITERION #2: DEFINE:

INTENT: Formulate the stakeholder problem. Define the problem, needs and objectives.

In my belief, the answer to this question is clearly defined:

5 Strongly Agree

4 Agree

3 Neutral

2 Disagree

1 Strongly Disagree

1. Has the direction changed at all during the course of Risk Committee? If so, when did it change and why?
<--- Score

2. Is the current 'as is' process being followed? If not, what are the discrepancies?
<--- Score

3. What constraints exist that might impact the team?

<--- Score

4. Will team members regularly document their Risk Committee work?
<--- Score

5. What are the tasks and definitions?
<--- Score

6. Are there any constraints known that bear on the ability to perform Risk Committee work? How is the team addressing them?
<--- Score

7. What are the Risk Committee use cases?
<--- Score

8. How have you defined all Risk Committee requirements first?
<--- Score

9. What are the Roles and Responsibilities for each team member and its leadership? Where is this documented?
<--- Score

10. Have all of the relationships been defined properly?
<--- Score

11. Has anyone else (internal or external to the group) attempted to solve this problem or a similar one before? If so, what knowledge can be leveraged from these previous efforts?
<--- Score

12. Has a high-level 'as is' process map been completed, verified and validated?
<--- Score

13. What is a worst-case scenario for losses?
<--- Score

14. What are the dynamics of the communication plan?
<--- Score

15. Are customer(s) identified and segmented according to their different needs and requirements?
<--- Score

16. Is the team sponsored by a champion or stakeholder leader?
<--- Score

17. Have specific policy objectives been defined?
<--- Score

18. How often are the team meetings?
<--- Score

19. When are meeting minutes sent out? Who is on the distribution list?
<--- Score

20. How do you manage scope?
<--- Score

21. How does the Risk Committee manager ensure against scope creep?
<--- Score

22. Is there a critical path to deliver Risk Committee results?
<--- Score

23. Are audit criteria, scope, frequency and methods defined?
<--- Score

24. What specifically is the problem? Where does it occur? When does it occur? What is its extent?
<--- Score

25. Do you have a Risk Committee success story or case study ready to tell and share?
<--- Score

26. What information should you gather?
<--- Score

27. What gets examined?
<--- Score

28. What baselines are required to be defined and managed?
<--- Score

29. Is the work to date meeting requirements?
<--- Score

30. What key stakeholder process output measure(s) does Risk Committee leverage and how?
<--- Score

31. Are accountability and ownership for Risk Committee clearly defined?
<--- Score

32. What are the core elements of the Risk Committee business case?
<--- Score

33. Are resources adequate for the scope?
<--- Score

34. Does the team have regular meetings?
<--- Score

35. What Risk Committee requirements should be gathered?
<--- Score

36. What are the boundaries of the scope? What is in bounds and what is not? What is the start point? What is the stop point?
<--- Score

37. How would you define the culture at your organization, how susceptible is it to Risk Committee changes?
<--- Score

38. What is the scope of the Risk Committee effort?
<--- Score

39. What knowledge or experience is required?
<--- Score

40. Is there a completed, verified, and validated high-level 'as is' (not 'should be' or 'could be') stakeholder process map?
<--- Score

41. Has your scope been defined?
<--- Score

42. How do you gather requirements?
<--- Score

43. How do you manage unclear Risk Committee requirements?
<--- Score

44. Do you all define Risk Committee in the same way?
<--- Score

45. What information do you gather?
<--- Score

46. Is there any additional Risk Committee definition of success?
<--- Score

47. What scope to assess?
<--- Score

48. Who is gathering information?
<--- Score

49. Is the team formed and are team leaders (Coaches and Management Leads) assigned?
<--- Score

50. How do you keep key subject matter experts in the loop?
<--- Score

51. Scope of sensitive information?
<--- Score

52. How do you gather Risk Committee requirements?
<--- Score

53. Who are the Risk Committee improvement team members, including Management Leads and Coaches?
<--- Score

54. How do you catch Risk Committee definition inconsistencies?
<--- Score

55. Who is gathering Risk Committee information?
<--- Score

56. What are the rough order estimates on cost savings/opportunities that Risk Committee brings?
<--- Score

57. Is the team equipped with available and reliable resources?
<--- Score

58. Is Risk Committee linked to key stakeholder goals and objectives?
<--- Score

59. Do the problem and goal statements meet the SMART criteria (specific, measurable, attainable, relevant, and time-bound)?
<--- Score

60. How and when will the baselines be defined?
<--- Score

61. What is out of scope?
<--- Score

62. Has a project plan, Gantt chart, or similar been developed/completed?
<--- Score

63. Are all requirements met?
<--- Score

64. Are required metrics defined, what are they?
<--- Score

65. What sources do you use to gather information for a Risk Committee study?
<--- Score

66. Have the customer needs been translated into specific, measurable requirements? How?
<--- Score

67. Are improvement team members fully trained on Risk Committee?
<--- Score

68. When is the estimated completion date?
<--- Score

69. Why are you doing Risk Committee and what is the scope?
<--- Score

70. Is there a completed SIPOC representation, describing the Suppliers, Inputs, Process, Outputs, and Customers?
<--- Score

71. Are the Risk Committee requirements complete?
<--- Score

72. What critical content must be communicated –
who, what, when, where, and how?
<--- Score

73. How do you gather the stories?
<--- Score

74. What Risk Committee services do you require?
<--- Score

75. Are roles and responsibilities formally defined?
<--- Score

76. How is the team tracking and documenting its
work?
<--- Score

77. How did the Risk Committee manager receive
input to the development of a Risk Committee
improvement plan and the estimated completion
dates/times of each activity?
<--- Score

78. What sort of initial information to gather?
<--- Score

79. Is data collected and displayed to better
understand customer(s) critical needs and
requirements.
<--- Score

80. What is out-of-scope initially?

<--- Score

81. What intelligence can you gather?
<--- Score

82. Is there a Risk Committee management charter, including stakeholder case, problem and goal statements, scope, milestones, roles and responsibilities, communication plan?
<--- Score

83. What is the definition of success?
<--- Score

84. How can the value of Risk Committee be defined?
<--- Score

85. Has everyone on the team, including the team leaders, been properly trained?
<--- Score

86. Is special Risk Committee user knowledge required?
<--- Score

87. What was the context?
<--- Score

88. Is the scope of Risk Committee defined?
<--- Score

89. Is Risk Committee currently on schedule according to the plan?
<--- Score

90. What is the scope of Risk Committee?

<--- Score

91. How do you build the right business case?
<--- Score

92. Are task requirements clearly defined?
<--- Score

93. How do you think the partners involved in Risk Committee would have defined success?
<--- Score

94. What are the compelling stakeholder reasons for embarking on Risk Committee?
<--- Score

95. How are consistent Risk Committee definitions important?
<--- Score

96. Has/have the customer(s) been identified?
<--- Score

97. How will variation in the actual durations of each activity be dealt with to ensure that the expected Risk Committee results are met?
<--- Score

98. Are there different segments of customers?
<--- Score

99. Is Risk Committee required?
<--- Score

100. Is scope creep really all bad news?
<--- Score

101. Is there regularly 100% attendance at the team meetings? If not, have appointed substitutes attended to preserve cross-functionality and full representation?
<--- Score

102. Will team members perform Risk Committee work when assigned and in a timely fashion?
<--- Score

103. What scope do you want your strategy to cover?
<--- Score

104. What is the scope of the Risk Committee work?
<--- Score

105. Is the Risk Committee scope complete and appropriately sized?
<--- Score

106. What are (control) requirements for Risk Committee Information?
<--- Score

107. Is the Risk Committee scope manageable?
<--- Score

108. What are the Risk Committee tasks and definitions?
<--- Score

109. What customer feedback methods were used to solicit their input?
<--- Score

110. Does the scope remain the same?
<--- Score

111. In what way can you redefine the criteria of choice clients have in your category in your favor?
<--- Score

112. Is there a clear Risk Committee case definition?
<--- Score

113. Are different versions of process maps needed to account for the different types of inputs?
<--- Score

114. Has a Risk Committee requirement not been met?
<--- Score

115. When is/was the Risk Committee start date?
<--- Score

116. How was the 'as is' process map developed, reviewed, verified and validated?
<--- Score

117. How would you define Risk Committee leadership?
<--- Score

118. What happens if Risk Committee's scope changes?
<--- Score

119. Have all basic functions of Risk Committee been defined?
<--- Score

120. What would be the goal or target for a Risk Committee's improvement team?
<--- Score

121. Is the team adequately staffed with the desired cross-functionality? If not, what additional resources are available to the team?
<--- Score

122. Do you have organizational privacy requirements?
<--- Score

123. Is the improvement team aware of the different versions of a process: what they think it is vs. what it actually is vs. what it should be vs. what it could be?
<--- Score

124. Has the improvement team collected the 'voice of the customer' (obtained feedback – qualitative and quantitative)?
<--- Score

125. Has a team charter been developed and communicated?
<--- Score

126. If substitutes have been appointed, have they been briefed on the Risk Committee goals and received regular communications as to the progress to date?
<--- Score

127. What are the requirements for audit information?
<--- Score

128. What is the context?
<--- Score

129. Has the Risk Committee work been fairly and/
or equitably divided and delegated among team
members who are qualified and capable to perform
the work? Has everyone contributed?
<--- Score

130. What are the record-keeping requirements of
Risk Committee activities?
<--- Score

131. Is full participation by members in regularly held
team meetings guaranteed?
<--- Score

132. What is the worst case scenario?
<--- Score

133. What is in scope?
<--- Score

134. How will the Risk Committee team and the group
measure complete success of Risk Committee?
<--- Score

135. Who approved the Risk Committee scope?
<--- Score

136. Where can you gather more information?
<--- Score

Add up total points for this section:
_ _ _ _ _ = Total points for this section

Divided by: _____ (number of
statements answered) = _____
Average score for this section

Transfer your score to the Risk
Committee Index at the beginning of the
Self-Assessment.

CRITERION #3: MEASURE:

In my belief, the answer to this
question is clearly defined:

5 Strongly Agree

4 Agree

3 Neutral

2 Disagree

1 Strongly Disagree

1. Are the units of measure consistent?
<--- Score

2. What are the types and number of measures to use?
<--- Score

3. What drives O&M cost?
<--- Score

4. How do you control the overall costs of your work processes?
<--- Score

5. Is the solution cost-effective?
<--- Score

6. How sensitive must the Risk Committee strategy be to cost?
<--- Score

7. What methods are feasible and acceptable to estimate the impact of reforms?
<--- Score

8. Are you able to realize any cost savings?
<--- Score

9. What is the total fixed cost?
<--- Score

10. What are the Risk Committee investment costs?
<--- Score

11. What measurements are possible, practicable and meaningful?
<--- Score

12. Does management have the right priorities among projects?
<--- Score

13. What are you verifying?
<--- Score

14. How do you measure lifecycle phases?

<--- Score

15. Does a Risk Committee quantification method exist?
<--- Score

16. What are your primary costs, revenues, assets?
<--- Score

17. How can you reduce costs?
<--- Score

18. How much does it cost?
<--- Score

19. What is the cost of rework?
<--- Score

20. What is the root cause(s) of the problem?
<--- Score

21. What evidence is there and what is measured?
<--- Score

22. How will success or failure be measured?
<--- Score

23. Among the Risk Committee product and service cost to be estimated, which is considered hardest to estimate?
<--- Score

24. What is an unallowable cost?
<--- Score

25. Do you have an issue in getting priority?

<--- Score

26. Are there competing Risk Committee priorities?
<--- Score

27. Has a cost center been established?
<--- Score

28. How do you measure success?
<--- Score

29. When should you bother with diagrams?
<--- Score

30. What is the total cost related to deploying Risk Committee, including any consulting or professional services?
<--- Score

31. What are the estimated costs of proposed changes?
<--- Score

32. What can be used to verify compliance?
<--- Score

33. Which costs should be taken into account?
<--- Score

34. Do you have a flow diagram of what happens?
<--- Score

35. Is the cost worth the Risk Committee effort ?
<--- Score

36. How are costs allocated?

<--- Score

37. Have you made assumptions about the shape of the future, particularly its impact on your customers and competitors?
<--- Score

38. Why do the measurements/indicators matter?
<--- Score

39. How do you verify performance?
<--- Score

40. Was a business case (cost/benefit) developed?
<--- Score

41. How can a Risk Committee test verify your ideas or assumptions?
<--- Score

42. What users will be impacted?
<--- Score

43. How can you measure the performance?
<--- Score

44. What is your Risk Committee quality cost segregation study?
<--- Score

45. Are the Risk Committee benefits worth its costs?
<--- Score

46. What is the Risk Committee business impact?
<--- Score

47. Have design-to-cost goals been established?
<--- Score

48. Who should receive measurement reports?
<--- Score

49. Are indirect costs charged to the Risk Committee program?
<--- Score

50. What are the costs of delaying Risk Committee action?
<--- Score

51. How are measurements made?
<--- Score

52. Why do you expend time and effort to implement measurement, for whom?
<--- Score

53. What do you measure and why?
<--- Score

54. Are Risk Committee vulnerabilities categorized and prioritized?
<--- Score

55. Does the Risk Committee task fit the client's priorities?
<--- Score

56. How can you reduce the costs of obtaining inputs?
<--- Score

57. What are the strategic priorities for this year?

<--- Score

58. How frequently do you track Risk Committee measures?
<--- Score

59. Are actual costs in line with budgeted costs?
<--- Score

60. Is it possible to estimate the impact of unanticipated complexity such as wrong or failed assumptions, feedback, etcetera on proposed reforms?
<--- Score

61. How will effects be measured?
<--- Score

62. What would it cost to replace your technology?
<--- Score

63. Where is it measured?
<--- Score

64. What causes investor action?
<--- Score

65. Do the benefits outweigh the costs?
<--- Score

66. What does your operating model cost?
<--- Score

67. Which measures and indicators matter?
<--- Score

68. When a disaster occurs, who gets priority?
<--- Score

69. Do you verify that corrective actions were taken?
<--- Score

70. What are hidden Risk Committee quality costs?
<--- Score

71. What are the uncertainties surrounding estimates of impact?
<--- Score

72. How do you verify if Risk Committee is built right?
<--- Score

73. What details are required of the Risk Committee cost structure?
<--- Score

74. What are the costs?
<--- Score

75. How do you verify your resources?
<--- Score

76. How do you verify the authenticity of the data and information used?
<--- Score

77. What is your decision requirements diagram?
<--- Score

78. How can you manage cost down?
<--- Score

79. What harm might be caused?
<--- Score

80. What potential environmental factors impact the Risk Committee effort?
<--- Score

81. Are you aware of what could cause a problem?
<--- Score

82. What measurements are being captured?
<--- Score

83. What tests verify requirements?
<--- Score

84. Where is the cost?
<--- Score

85. Do you effectively measure and reward individual and team performance?
<--- Score

86. How will measures be used to manage and adapt?
<--- Score

87. Are the measurements objective?
<--- Score

88. What happens if cost savings do not materialize?
<--- Score

89. What relevant entities could be measured?
<--- Score

90. Do you aggressively reward and promote the

people who have the biggest impact on creating excellent Risk Committee services/products?
<--- Score

91. What causes innovation to fail or succeed in your organization?
<--- Score

92. What disadvantage does this cause for the user?
<--- Score

93. What are allowable costs?
<--- Score

94. How is performance measured?
<--- Score

95. What does a Test Case verify?
<--- Score

96. How do you aggregate measures across priorities?
<--- Score

97. How is the value delivered by Risk Committee being measured?
<--- Score

98. What are the operational costs after Risk Committee deployment?
<--- Score

99. Are there any easy-to-implement alternatives to Risk Committee? Sometimes other solutions are available that do not require the cost implications of a full-blown project?
<--- Score

100. Will Risk Committee have an impact on current business continuity, disaster recovery processes and/or infrastructure?
<--- Score

101. How do you verify the Risk Committee requirements quality?
<--- Score

102. Who pays the cost?
<--- Score

103. When are costs are incurred?
<--- Score

104. How will your organization measure success?
<--- Score

105. How do you quantify and qualify impacts?
<--- Score

106. What are the costs and benefits?
<--- Score

107. What could cause delays in the schedule?
<--- Score

108. How will you measure success?
<--- Score

109. How is progress measured?
<--- Score

110. Which Risk Committee impacts are significant?
<--- Score

111. How long to keep data and how to manage retention costs?
<--- Score

112. What do people want to verify?
<--- Score

113. How do you prevent mis-estimating cost?
<--- Score

114. How do you measure efficient delivery of Risk Committee services?
<--- Score

115. How do you verify and develop ideas and innovations?
<--- Score

116. How do you verify and validate the Risk Committee data?
<--- Score

117. How will costs be allocated?
<--- Score

118. How can you measure Risk Committee in a systematic way?
<--- Score

119. What are the Risk Committee key cost drivers?
<--- Score

120. What are the costs of reform?
<--- Score

121. What causes mismanagement?
<--- Score

122. Did you tackle the cause or the symptom?
<--- Score

123. What are your key Risk Committee organizational performance measures, including key short and longer-term financial measures?
<--- Score

124. What is the cause of any Risk Committee gaps?
<--- Score

125. At what cost?
<--- Score

126. Have you included everything in your Risk Committee cost models?
<--- Score

127. Where can you go to verify the info?
<--- Score

128. Is there an opportunity to verify requirements?
<--- Score

129. What does losing customers cost your organization?
<--- Score

130. Are supply costs steady or fluctuating?
<--- Score

131. What are the current costs of the Risk Committee process?

<--- Score

132. What could cause you to change course?
<--- Score

133. What are your customers expectations and measures?
<--- Score

134. Are missed Risk Committee opportunities costing your organization money?
<--- Score

135. Do you have any cost Risk Committee limitation requirements?
<--- Score

136. What are your operating costs?
<--- Score

137. How do your measurements capture actionable Risk Committee information for use in exceeding your customers expectations and securing your customers engagement?
<--- Score

138. Are you taking your company in the direction of better and revenue or cheaper and cost?
<--- Score

Add up total points for this section:
_ _ _ _ _ = Total points for this section

Divided by: _ _ _ _ _ _ (number of statements answered) = _ _ _ _ _ _
Average score for this section

Transfer your score to the Risk
Committee Index at the beginning of the
Self-Assessment.

CRITERION #4: ANALYZE:

INTENT: Analyze causes, assumptions and hypotheses.

In my belief, the answer to this question is clearly defined:

5 Strongly Agree

4 Agree

3 Neutral

2 Disagree

1 Strongly Disagree

1. Did any additional data need to be collected?
<--- Score

2. What are the disruptive Risk Committee technologies that enable your organization to radically change your business processes?
<--- Score

3. Are Risk Committee changes recognized early enough to be approved through the regular process?

<--- Score

4. Is pre-qualification of suppliers carried out?
<--- Score

5. How do you identify specific Risk Committee investment opportunities and emerging trends?
<--- Score

6. How do you ensure that the Risk Committee opportunity is realistic?
<--- Score

7. What do you need to qualify?
<--- Score

8. What, related to, Risk Committee processes does your organization outsource?
<--- Score

9. How do you measure the operational performance of your key work systems and processes, including productivity, cycle time, and other appropriate measures of process effectiveness, efficiency, and innovation?
<--- Score

10. How has the Risk Committee data been gathered?
<--- Score

11. What conclusions were drawn from the team's data collection and analysis? How did the team reach these conclusions?
<--- Score

12. What is the cost of poor quality as supported by

the team's analysis?
<--- Score

13. What Risk Committee data will be collected?
<--- Score

14. Which Risk Committee data should be retained?
<--- Score

15. What did the team gain from developing a sub-process map?
<--- Score

16. What internal processes need improvement?
<--- Score

17. Do your contracts/agreements contain data security obligations?
<--- Score

18. What is the Value Stream Mapping?
<--- Score

19. Have any additional benefits been identified that will result from closing all or most of the gaps?
<--- Score

20. Has data output been validated?
<--- Score

21. How can risk management be tied procedurally to process elements?
<--- Score

22. Record-keeping requirements flow from the records needed as inputs, outputs, controls and for

transformation of a Risk Committee process, are the records needed as inputs to the Risk Committee process available?
<--- Score

23. Who gets your output?
<--- Score

24. Where can you get qualified talent today?
<--- Score

25. What are your best practices for minimizing Risk Committee project risk, while demonstrating incremental value and quick wins throughout the Risk Committee project lifecycle?
<--- Score

26. How much data can be collected in the given timeframe?
<--- Score

27. Is data and process analysis, root cause analysis and quantifying the gap/opportunity in place?
<--- Score

28. How does the organization define, manage, and improve its Risk Committee processes?
<--- Score

29. What is the output?
<--- Score

30. Do your leaders quickly bounce back from setbacks?
<--- Score

31. Is there a strict change management process?
<--- Score

32. How is the Risk Committee Value Stream Mapping managed?
<--- Score

33. What systems/processes must you excel at?
<--- Score

34. Think about some of the processes you undertake within your organization, which do you own?
<--- Score

35. What Risk Committee data should be collected?
<--- Score

36. What process improvements will be needed?
<--- Score

37. How many input/output points does it require?
<--- Score

38. Do staff qualifications match your project?
<--- Score

39. What are the Risk Committee business drivers?
<--- Score

40. Has an output goal been set?
<--- Score

41. Are you missing Risk Committee opportunities?
<--- Score

42. How is Risk Committee data gathered?

<--- Score

43. Who is involved in the management review process?
<--- Score

44. How do mission and objectives affect the Risk Committee processes of your organization?
<--- Score

45. What are your outputs?
<--- Score

46. What will drive Risk Committee change?
<--- Score

47. What successful thing are you doing today that may be blinding you to new growth opportunities?
<--- Score

48. What are the necessary qualifications?
<--- Score

49. What Risk Committee data should be managed?
<--- Score

50. How do you implement and manage your work processes to ensure that they meet design requirements?
<--- Score

51. What qualifications are needed?
<--- Score

52. What are the Risk Committee design outputs?
<--- Score

53. Should you invest in industry-recognized qualifications?
<--- Score

54. What are the processes for audit reporting and management?
<--- Score

55. Identify an operational issue in your organization, for example, could a particular task be done more quickly or more efficiently by Risk Committee?
<--- Score

56. Who is involved with workflow mapping?
<--- Score

57. What are your current levels and trends in key measures or indicators of Risk Committee product and process performance that are important to and directly serve your customers? How do these results compare with the performance of your competitors and other organizations with similar offerings?
<--- Score

58. Do several people in different organizational units assist with the Risk Committee process?
<--- Score

59. What resources go in to get the desired output?
<--- Score

60. How are outputs preserved and protected?
<--- Score

61. What are evaluation criteria for the output?

<--- Score

62. Can you add value to the current Risk Committee decision-making process (largely qualitative) by incorporating uncertainty modeling (more quantitative)?
<--- Score

63. What were the financial benefits resulting from any 'ground fruit or low-hanging fruit' (quick fixes)?
<--- Score

64. What kind of crime could a potential new hire have committed that would not only not disqualify him/her from being hired by your organization, but would actually indicate that he/she might be a particularly good fit?
<--- Score

65. What Risk Committee metrics are outputs of the process?
<--- Score

66. Who owns what data?
<--- Score

67. How is the way you as the leader think and process information affecting your organizational culture?
<--- Score

68. What types of data do your Risk Committee indicators require?
<--- Score

69. What are your key performance measures or indicators and in-process measures for the control

and improvement of your Risk Committee processes?
<--- Score

70. When should a process be art not science?
<--- Score

71. What are the personnel training and qualifications required?
<--- Score

72. Were there any improvement opportunities identified from the process analysis?
<--- Score

73. What qualifications do Risk Committee leaders need?
<--- Score

74. Think about the functions involved in your Risk Committee project, what processes flow from these functions?
<--- Score

75. Was a cause-and-effect diagram used to explore the different types of causes (or sources of variation)?
<--- Score

76. Did any value-added analysis or 'lean thinking' take place to identify some of the gaps shown on the 'as is' process map?
<--- Score

77. What controls do you have in place to protect data?
<--- Score

78. Do your employees have the opportunity to do what they do best everyday?
<--- Score

79. Who will gather what data?
<--- Score

80. Do you, as a leader, bounce back quickly from setbacks?
<--- Score

81. What qualifications and skills do you need?
<--- Score

82. What other organizational variables, such as reward systems or communication systems, affect the performance of this Risk Committee process?
<--- Score

83. What is the Risk Committee Driver?
<--- Score

84. Do you have the authority to produce the output?
<--- Score

85. How will the Risk Committee data be captured?
<--- Score

86. How do you define collaboration and team output?
<--- Score

87. What is the complexity of the output produced?
<--- Score

88. Were Pareto charts (or similar) used to portray the

'heavy hitters' (or key sources of variation)?
<--- Score

89. Who qualifies to gain access to data?
<--- Score

90. How do your work systems and key work processes relate to and capitalize on your core competencies?
<--- Score

91. How often will data be collected for measures?
<--- Score

92. Is there an established change management process?
<--- Score

93. Is there any way to speed up the process?
<--- Score

94. What quality tools were used to get through the analyze phase?
<--- Score

95. What tools were used to generate the list of possible causes?
<--- Score

96. What is your organizations system for selecting qualified vendors?
<--- Score

97. Have you defined which data is gathered how?
<--- Score

98. Is the final output clearly identified?
<--- Score

99. What are your current levels and trends in key Risk Committee measures or indicators of product and process performance that are important to and directly serve your customers?
<--- Score

100. Who will facilitate the team and process?
<--- Score

101. How will corresponding data be collected?
<--- Score

102. Is the Risk Committee process severely broken such that a re-design is necessary?
<--- Score

103. How will the data be checked for quality?
<--- Score

104. What is your organizations process which leads to recognition of value generation?
<--- Score

105. How was the detailed process map generated, verified, and validated?
<--- Score

106. Are all team members qualified for all tasks?
<--- Score

107. What data do you need to collect?
<--- Score

108. What methods do you use to gather Risk Committee data?
<--- Score

109. Is the performance gap determined?
<--- Score

110. Do you understand your management processes today?
<--- Score

111. Were any designed experiments used to generate additional insight into the data analysis?
<--- Score

112. A compounding model resolution with available relevant data can often provide insight towards a solution methodology; which Risk Committee models, tools and techniques are necessary?
<--- Score

113. What does the data say about the performance of the stakeholder process?
<--- Score

114. What Risk Committee data do you gather or use now?
<--- Score

115. Do quality systems drive continuous improvement?
<--- Score

116. How do you promote understanding that opportunity for improvement is not criticism of the status quo, or the people who created the status quo?

<--- Score

117. Have the problem and goal statements been updated to reflect the additional knowledge gained from the analyze phase?
<--- Score

118. What information qualified as important?
<--- Score

119. How do you use Risk Committee data and information to support organizational decision making and innovation?
<--- Score

120. What qualifications are necessary?
<--- Score

121. How difficult is it to qualify what Risk Committee ROI is?
<--- Score

122. Are all staff in core Risk Committee subjects Highly Qualified?
<--- Score

123. What data is gathered?
<--- Score

124. Is the required Risk Committee data gathered?
<--- Score

125. What qualifies as competition?
<--- Score

126. Is the gap/opportunity displayed and

communicated in financial terms?
<--- Score

127. What training and qualifications will you need?
<--- Score

128. How is the data gathered?
<--- Score

129. What tools were used to narrow the list of possible causes?
<--- Score

130. What were the crucial 'moments of truth' on the process map?
<--- Score

131. Is the suppliers process defined and controlled?
<--- Score

132. What are the best opportunities for value improvement?
<--- Score

133. What are the revised rough estimates of the financial savings/opportunity for Risk Committee improvements?
<--- Score

134. Was a detailed process map created to amplify critical steps of the 'as is' stakeholder process?
<--- Score

135. Are gaps between current performance and the goal performance identified?
<--- Score

136. Where is the data coming from to measure compliance?
<--- Score

137. What other jobs or tasks affect the performance of the steps in the Risk Committee process?
<--- Score

138. How is data used for program management and improvement?
<--- Score

139. Are your outputs consistent?
<--- Score

Add up total points for this section:
_ _ _ _ _ = Total points for this section

Divided by: _ _ _ _ _ _ (number of statements answered) = _ _ _ _ _ _
Average score for this section

Transfer your score to the Risk Committee Index at the beginning of the Self-Assessment.

CRITERION #5: IMPROVE:

INTENT: Develop a practical solution. Innovate, establish and test the solution and to measure the results.

In my belief, the answer to this question is clearly defined:

5 Strongly Agree

4 Agree

3 Neutral

2 Disagree

1 Strongly Disagree

1. What resources are required for the improvement efforts?
<--- Score

2. Have you identified breakpoints and/or risk tolerances that will trigger broad consideration of a potential need for intervention or modification of strategy?
<--- Score

3. How are policy decisions made and where?
<--- Score

4. Are risk management tasks balanced centrally and locally?
<--- Score

5. What alternative responses are available to manage risk?
<--- Score

6. Who will be responsible for making the decisions to include or exclude requested changes once Risk Committee is underway?
<--- Score

7. Is Risk Committee documentation maintained?
<--- Score

8. At what point will vulnerability assessments be performed once Risk Committee is put into production (e.g., ongoing Risk Management after implementation)?
<--- Score

9. Can the solution be designed and implemented within an acceptable time period?
<--- Score

10. Are events managed to resolution?
<--- Score

11. Do you have the optimal project management team structure?
<--- Score

12. In the past few months, what is the smallest change you have made that has had the biggest positive result? What was it about that small change that produced the large return?
<--- Score

13. Have you achieved Risk Committee improvements?
<--- Score

14. How do you manage Risk Committee risk?
<--- Score

15. How do you improve Risk Committee service perception, and satisfaction?
<--- Score

16. How do you improve your likelihood of success ?
<--- Score

17. Which of the recognised risks out of all risks can be most likely transferred?
<--- Score

18. What should a proof of concept or pilot accomplish?
<--- Score

19. Where do the Risk Committee decisions reside?
<--- Score

20. What criteria will you use to assess your Risk Committee risks?
<--- Score

21. Is the scope clearly documented?
<--- Score

22. How does your organization evaluate strategic Risk Committee success?
<--- Score

23. Do you cover the five essential competencies: Communication, Collaboration,Innovation, Adaptability, and Leadership that improve an organizations ability to leverage the new Risk Committee in a volatile global economy?
<--- Score

24. Why improve in the first place?
<--- Score

25. Is risk periodically assessed?
<--- Score

26. Who makes the Risk Committee decisions in your organization?
<--- Score

27. How will you measure the results?
<--- Score

28. What are the implications of the one critical Risk Committee decision 10 minutes, 10 months, and 10 years from now?
<--- Score

29. How do you keep improving Risk Committee?
<--- Score

30. Are the most efficient solutions problem-specific?

<--- Score

31. Who are the people involved in developing and implementing Risk Committee?
<--- Score

32. How risky is your organization?
<--- Score

33. How do you define the solutions' scope?
<--- Score

34. Who are the Risk Committee decision makers?
<--- Score

35. What current systems have to be understood and/ or changed?
<--- Score

36. How can skill-level changes improve Risk Committee?
<--- Score

37. Who will be using the results of the measurement activities?
<--- Score

38. What assumptions are made about the solution and approach?
<--- Score

39. Are you assessing Risk Committee and risk?
<--- Score

40. Is there a high likelihood that any recommendations will achieve their intended results?

<--- Score

41. If you could go back in time five years, what decision would you make differently? What is your best guess as to what decision you're making today you might regret five years from now?
<--- Score

42. How do you improve productivity?
<--- Score

43. How do you link measurement and risk?
<--- Score

44. Explorations of the frontiers of Risk Committee will help you build influence, improve Risk Committee, optimize decision making, and sustain change, what is your approach?
<--- Score

45. Does a good decision guarantee a good outcome?
<--- Score

46. Can you identify any significant risks or exposures to Risk Committee third- parties (vendors, service providers, alliance partners etc) that concern you?
<--- Score

47. How can you improve Risk Committee?
<--- Score

48. Who controls the risk?
<--- Score

49. Who will be responsible for documenting the Risk Committee requirements in detail?

<--- Score

50. What is the Risk Committee's sustainability risk?
<--- Score

51. What actually has to improve and by how much?
<--- Score

52. Are the key business and technology risks being managed?
<--- Score

53. Where do you need Risk Committee improvement?
<--- Score

54. Does the goal represent a desired result that can be measured?
<--- Score

55. Which Risk Committee solution is appropriate?
<--- Score

56. Who are the Risk Committee decision-makers?
<--- Score

57. How do the Risk Committee results compare with the performance of your competitors and other organizations with similar offerings?
<--- Score

58. How do you deal with Risk Committee risk?
<--- Score

59. Risk events: what are the things that could go wrong?

<--- Score

60. How will you know that you have improved?
<--- Score

61. How do you decide how much to remunerate an employee?
<--- Score

62. What do you want to improve?
<--- Score

63. Is the Risk Committee solution sustainable?
<--- Score

64. Was a Risk Committee charter developed?
<--- Score

65. How do you measure progress and evaluate training effectiveness?
<--- Score

66. What needs improvement? Why?
<--- Score

67. Is supporting Risk Committee documentation required?
<--- Score

68. Are the risks fully understood, reasonable and manageable?
<--- Score

69. What area needs the greatest improvement?
<--- Score

70. How is knowledge sharing about risk management improved?
<--- Score

71. Who should make the Risk Committee decisions?
<--- Score

72. What went well, what should change, what can improve?
<--- Score

73. For decision problems, how do you develop a decision statement?
<--- Score

74. How scalable is your Risk Committee solution?
<--- Score

75. How significant is the improvement in the eyes of the end user?
<--- Score

76. How does the team improve its work?
<--- Score

77. Is there any other Risk Committee solution?
<--- Score

78. Who do you report Risk Committee results to?
<--- Score

79. How is continuous improvement applied to risk management?
<--- Score

80. Are procedures documented for managing Risk

Committee risks?
<--- Score

81. What is the magnitude of the improvements?
<--- Score

82. What Risk Committee improvements can be made?
<--- Score

83. Do you have a risk register / risk committee?
<--- Score

84. Is the Risk Committee risk managed?
<--- Score

85. Do you currently have a Risk Committee or are the already stated governance functions carried out by existing committees of the Board?
<--- Score

86. Is the Risk Committee documentation thorough?
<--- Score

87. Do those selected for the Risk Committee team have a good general understanding of what Risk Committee is all about?
<--- Score

88. How are Risk Committee risks managed?
<--- Score

89. How can the phases of Risk Committee development be identified?
<--- Score

90. How will you recognize and celebrate results?
<--- Score

91. What are the concrete Risk Committee results?
<--- Score

92. What are your current levels and trends in key measures or indicators of workforce and leader development?
<--- Score

93. How will you know when its improved?
<--- Score

94. What is Risk Committee risk?
<--- Score

95. Do vendor agreements bring new compliance risk ?
<--- Score

96. What are the expected Risk Committee results?
<--- Score

97. Who manages supplier risk management in your organization?
<--- Score

98. When you map the key players in your own work and the types/domains of relationships with them, which relationships do you find easy and which challenging, and why?
<--- Score

99. How will you know that a change is an improvement?

<--- Score

100. Is the measure of success for Risk Committee understandable to a variety of people?
<--- Score

101. What tools do you use once you have decided on a Risk Committee strategy and more importantly how do you choose?
<--- Score

102. How can you better manage risk?
<--- Score

103. Risk Committee risk decisions: whose call Is It?
<--- Score

104. Who are the key stakeholders for the Risk Committee evaluation?
<--- Score

105. Does your organization have a Board Risk Committee?
<--- Score

106. What to do with the results or outcomes of measurements?
<--- Score

107. What are the Risk Committee security risks?
<--- Score

108. Risk factors: what are the characteristics of Risk Committee that make it risky?
<--- Score

109. How do you measure improved Risk Committee service perception, and satisfaction?
<--- Score

110. What improvements have been achieved?
<--- Score

111. Is the solution technically practical?
<--- Score

112. Is any Risk Committee documentation required?
<--- Score

113. What were the criteria for evaluating a Risk Committee pilot?
<--- Score

114. How do you mitigate Risk Committee risk?
<--- Score

115. What is the risk?
<--- Score

116. For estimation problems, how do you develop an estimation statement?
<--- Score

117. How can you improve performance?
<--- Score

118. Do you have a Risk Committee at the board level or within management?
<--- Score

119. Who controls key decisions that will be made?
<--- Score

120. Are decisions made in a timely manner?
<--- Score

121. What were the underlying assumptions on the cost-benefit analysis?
<--- Score

122. What risks do you need to manage?
<--- Score

123. What are the affordable Risk Committee risks?
<--- Score

124. Do you need to do a usability evaluation?
<--- Score

125. Does you have a Risk Committee at the board level or within management?
<--- Score

126. Can you integrate quality management and risk management?
<--- Score

127. Do you combine technical expertise with business knowledge and Risk Committee Key topics include lifecycles, development approaches, requirements and how to make a business case?
<--- Score

128. What can you do to improve?
<--- Score

129. Are risk triggers captured?
<--- Score

130. What practices helps your organization to develop its capacity to recognize patterns?
<--- Score

131. Risk Identification: What are the possible risk events your organization faces in relation to Risk Committee?
<--- Score

Add up total points for this section:
_ _ _ _ _ = Total points for this section

Divided by: _ _ _ _ _ _ (number of statements answered) = _ _ _ _ _ _
Average score for this section

Transfer your score to the Risk Committee Index at the beginning of the Self-Assessment.

CRITERION #6: CONTROL:

INTENT: Implement the practical solution. Maintain the performance and correct possible complications.

In my belief, the answer to this question is clearly defined:

5 Strongly Agree

4 Agree

3 Neutral

2 Disagree

1 Strongly Disagree

1. Who is the Risk Committee process owner?
<--- Score

2. What do you measure to verify effectiveness gains?
<--- Score

3. What quality tools were useful in the control phase?
<--- Score

4. Is there a standardized process?
<--- Score

5. How will the process owner and team be able to hold the gains?
<--- Score

6. Is there documentation that will support the successful operation of the improvement?
<--- Score

7. Does job training on the documented procedures need to be part of the process team's education and training?
<--- Score

8. What do you stand for--and what are you against?
<--- Score

9. What are the key elements of your Risk Committee performance improvement system, including your evaluation, organizational learning, and innovation processes?
<--- Score

10. Is reporting being used or needed?
<--- Score

11. Does the Risk Committee performance meet the customer's requirements?
<--- Score

12. How might the group capture best practices and lessons learned so as to leverage improvements?
<--- Score

13. What key inputs and outputs are being measured on an ongoing basis?
<--- Score

14. What should the next improvement project be that is related to Risk Committee?
<--- Score

15. How do you encourage people to take control and responsibility?
<--- Score

16. Who is going to spread your message?
<--- Score

17. What is the recommended frequency of auditing?
<--- Score

18. How is change control managed?
<--- Score

19. How will the process owner verify improvement in present and future sigma levels, process capabilities?
<--- Score

20. Will any special training be provided for results interpretation?
<--- Score

21. How will report readings be checked to effectively monitor performance?
<--- Score

22. Who has control over resources?
<--- Score

23. Do the Risk Committee decisions you make today help people and the planet tomorrow?
<--- Score

24. How do you establish and deploy modified action plans if circumstances require a shift in plans and rapid execution of new plans?
<--- Score

25. What are you attempting to measure/monitor?
<--- Score

26. Is a response plan established and deployed?
<--- Score

27. How will Risk Committee decisions be made and monitored?
<--- Score

28. How will the day-to-day responsibilities for monitoring and continual improvement be transferred from the improvement team to the process owner?
<--- Score

29. What is the best design framework for Risk Committee organization now that, in a post industrial-age if the top-down, command and control model is no longer relevant?
<--- Score

30. What do your reports reflect?
<--- Score

31. Is there a control plan in place for sustaining improvements (short and long-term)?

<--- Score

32. How do your controls stack up?
<--- Score

33. What are the known security controls?
<--- Score

34. Is new knowledge gained imbedded in the response plan?
<--- Score

35. Does Risk Committee appropriately measure and monitor risk?
<--- Score

36. What is your theory of human motivation, and how does your compensation plan fit with that view?
<--- Score

37. Can you adapt and adjust to changing Risk Committee situations?
<--- Score

38. How do controls support value?
<--- Score

39. Are suggested corrective/restorative actions indicated on the response plan for known causes to problems that might surface?
<--- Score

40. Are you measuring, monitoring and predicting Risk Committee activities to optimize operations and profitability, and enhancing outcomes?
<--- Score

41. How is Risk Committee project cost planned, managed, monitored?
<--- Score

42. How will input, process, and output variables be checked to detect for sub-optimal conditions?
<--- Score

43. What are your results for key measures or indicators of the accomplishment of your Risk Committee strategy and action plans, including building and strengthening core competencies?
<--- Score

44. Do you monitor the effectiveness of your Risk Committee activities?
<--- Score

45. Is the Risk Committee test/monitoring cost justified?
<--- Score

46. Are operating procedures consistent?
<--- Score

47. What is the control/monitoring plan?
<--- Score

48. Is knowledge gained on process shared and institutionalized?
<--- Score

49. Do you monitor the Risk Committee decisions made and fine tune them as they evolve?
<--- Score

50. How do you select, collect, align, and integrate Risk Committee data and information for tracking daily operations and overall organizational performance, including progress relative to strategic objectives and action plans?
<--- Score

51. Do the viable solutions scale to future needs?
<--- Score

52. Are controls in place and consistently applied?
<--- Score

53. How do you plan on providing proper recognition and disclosure of supporting companies?
<--- Score

54. What adjustments to the strategies are needed?
<--- Score

55. How will you measure your QA plan's effectiveness?
<--- Score

56. How will new or emerging customer needs/ requirements be checked/communicated to orient the process toward meeting the new specifications and continually reducing variation?
<--- Score

57. What are the critical parameters to watch?
<--- Score

58. Will existing staff require re-training, for example, to learn new business processes?

<--- Score

59. Is there a transfer of ownership and knowledge to process owner and process team tasked with the responsibilities.
<--- Score

60. Is a response plan in place for when the input, process, or output measures indicate an 'out-of-control' condition?
<--- Score

61. How do senior leaders actions reflect a commitment to the organizations Risk Committee values?
<--- Score

62. Is there a recommended audit plan for routine surveillance inspections of Risk Committee's gains?
<--- Score

63. How do you spread information?
<--- Score

64. What Risk Committee standards are applicable?
<--- Score

65. Are the planned controls working?
<--- Score

66. Implementation Planning: is a pilot needed to test the changes before a full roll out occurs?
<--- Score

67. Are pertinent alerts monitored, analyzed and distributed to appropriate personnel?

<--- Score

68. What other areas of the group might benefit from the Risk Committee team's improvements, knowledge, and learning?
<--- Score

69. How likely is the current Risk Committee plan to come in on schedule or on budget?
<--- Score

70. What is your plan to assess your security risks?
<--- Score

71. Who will be in control?
<--- Score

72. What other systems, operations, processes, and infrastructures (hiring practices, staffing, training, incentives/rewards, metrics/dashboards/scorecards, etc.) need updates, additions, changes, or deletions in order to facilitate knowledge transfer and improvements?
<--- Score

73. Is there an action plan in case of emergencies?
<--- Score

74. Who controls critical resources?
<--- Score

75. Are the Risk Committee standards challenging?
<--- Score

76. Against what alternative is success being measured?

<--- Score

77. Are there documented procedures?
<--- Score

78. What are the performance and scale of the Risk Committee tools?
<--- Score

79. Does a troubleshooting guide exist or is it needed?
<--- Score

80. Is there a documented and implemented monitoring plan?
<--- Score

81. You may have created your quality measures at a time when you lacked resources, technology wasn't up to the required standard, or low service levels were the industry norm. Have those circumstances changed?
<--- Score

82. Are new process steps, standards, and documentation ingrained into normal operations?
<--- Score

83. What should you measure to verify efficiency gains?
<--- Score

84. What can you control?
<--- Score

85. How do you plan for the cost of succession?
<--- Score

86. Is there a Risk Committee Communication plan covering who needs to get what information when?
<--- Score

87. Has the Risk Committee value of standards been quantified?
<--- Score

88. Has the improved process and its steps been standardized?
<--- Score

89. How widespread is its use?
<--- Score

90. Does the response plan contain a definite closed loop continual improvement scheme (e.g., plan-do-check-act)?
<--- Score

91. Are the planned controls in place?
<--- Score

92. Act/Adjust: What Do you Need to Do Differently?
<--- Score

93. Are documented procedures clear and easy to follow for the operators?
<--- Score

94. What are customers monitoring?
<--- Score

95. In the case of a Risk Committee project, the criteria for the audit derive from implementation objectives,

an audit of a Risk Committee project involves assessing whether the recommendations outlined for implementation have been met, can you track that any Risk Committee project is implemented as planned, and is it working?
<--- Score

96. Have new or revised work instructions resulted?
<--- Score

Add up total points for this section:
_ _ _ _ _ = Total points for this section

Divided by: _ _ _ _ _ _ (number of statements answered) = _ _ _ _ _ _
Average score for this section

Transfer your score to the Risk Committee Index at the beginning of the Self-Assessment.

CRITERION #7: SUSTAIN:

INTENT: Retain the benefits.

In my belief, the answer to this question is clearly defined:

5 Strongly Agree

4 Agree

3 Neutral

2 Disagree

1 Strongly Disagree

1. What is your formula for success in Risk Committee ?
<--- Score

2. Do you think you know, or do you know you know ?
<--- Score

3. Is Risk Committee realistic, or are you setting yourself up for failure?
<--- Score

4. Can you do all this work?
<--- Score

5. What is something you believe that nearly no one agrees with you on?
<--- Score

6. Is there a work around that you can use?
<--- Score

7. Will it be accepted by users?
<--- Score

8. What you are going to do to affect the numbers?
<--- Score

9. Marketing budgets are tighter, consumers are more skeptical, and social media has changed forever the way we talk about Risk Committee, how do you gain traction?
<--- Score

10. What trophy do you want on your mantle?
<--- Score

11. What is the craziest thing you can do?
<--- Score

12. Think of your Risk Committee project, what are the main functions?
<--- Score

13. What one word do you want to own in the minds of your customers, employees, and partners?
<--- Score

14. What did you miss in the interview for the worst hire you ever made?
<--- Score

15. What relationships among Risk Committee trends do you perceive?
<--- Score

16. How do you set Risk Committee stretch targets and how do you get people to not only participate in setting these stretch targets but also that they strive to achieve these?
<--- Score

17. Who will provide the final approval of Risk Committee deliverables?
<--- Score

18. Are the criteria for selecting recommendations stated?
<--- Score

19. Do you have the right capabilities and capacities?
<--- Score

20. Which models, tools and techniques are necessary?
<--- Score

21. What is your BATNA (best alternative to a negotiated agreement)?
<--- Score

22. What happens if you do not have enough funding?
<--- Score

23. Why should people listen to you?
<--- Score

24. What are the gaps in your knowledge and experience?
<--- Score

25. What is the overall business strategy?
<--- Score

26. What have you done to protect your business from competitive encroachment?
<--- Score

27. Operational - will it work?
<--- Score

28. Are you making progress, and are you making progress as Risk Committee leaders?
<--- Score

29. How do you govern and fulfill your societal responsibilities?
<--- Score

30. What are you challenging?
<--- Score

31. Who do you think the world wants your organization to be?
<--- Score

32. Can the schedule be done in the given time?
<--- Score

33. What should you stop doing?
<--- Score

34. What happens when a new employee joins the organization?
<--- Score

35. Who do you want your customers to become?
<--- Score

36. What would you recommend your friend do if he/ she were facing this dilemma?
<--- Score

37. What is the recommended frequency of auditing?
<--- Score

38. How do you foster innovation?
<--- Score

39. If you do not follow, then how to lead?
<--- Score

40. How can you incorporate support to ensure safe and effective use of Risk Committee into the services that you provide?
<--- Score

41. Why is it important to have senior management support for a Risk Committee project?
<--- Score

42. Are all key stakeholders present at all Structured Walkthroughs?
<--- Score

43. At what moment would you think; Will I get fired?
<--- Score

44. What are the top 3 things at the forefront of your Risk Committee agendas for the next 3 years?
<--- Score

45. Is the Risk Committee organization completing tasks effectively and efficiently?
<--- Score

46. Who are your customers?
<--- Score

47. Are the assumptions believable and achievable?
<--- Score

48. How do you manage Risk Committee Knowledge Management (KM)?
<--- Score

49. Who are four people whose careers you have enhanced?
<--- Score

50. What unique value proposition (UVP) do you offer?
<--- Score

51. How will you insure seamless interoperability of Risk Committee moving forward?
<--- Score

52. What is a feasible sequencing of reform initiatives over time?
<--- Score

53. Is Risk Committee dependent on the successful delivery of a current project?
<--- Score

54. How do you foster the skills, knowledge, talents, attributes, and characteristics you want to have?
<--- Score

55. What may be the consequences for the performance of an organization if all stakeholders are not consulted regarding Risk Committee?
<--- Score

56. What happens at your organization when people fail?
<--- Score

57. Who will be responsible for deciding whether Risk Committee goes ahead or not after the initial investigations?
<--- Score

58. Are assumptions made in Risk Committee stated explicitly?
<--- Score

59. How do you know if you are successful?
<--- Score

60. How do senior leaders deploy your organizations vision and values through your leadership system, to the workforce, to key suppliers and partners, and to customers and other stakeholders, as appropriate?
<--- Score

61. What are the short and long-term Risk Committee

goals?

<--- Score

62. Is your basic point _____ or _____?

<--- Score

63. Who uses your product in ways you never expected?

<--- Score

64. How do you create buy-in?

<--- Score

65. What projects are going on in the organization today, and what resources are those projects using from the resource pools?

<--- Score

66. Why is Risk Committee important for you now?

<--- Score

67. Is maximizing Risk Committee protection the same as minimizing Risk Committee loss?

<--- Score

68. What could happen if you do not do it?

<--- Score

69. What is it like to work for you?

<--- Score

70. When information truly is ubiquitous, when reach and connectivity are completely global, when computing resources are infinite, and when a whole new set of impossibilities are not only possible, but happening, what will that do to your business?

<--- Score

71. What is the estimated value of the project?
<--- Score

72. What are strategies for increasing support and reducing opposition?
<--- Score

73. Who will determine interim and final deadlines?
<--- Score

74. What is the range of capabilities?
<--- Score

75. What are you trying to prove to yourself, and how might it be hijacking your life and business success?
<--- Score

76. How do you make it meaningful in connecting Risk Committee with what users do day-to-day?
<--- Score

77. What goals did you miss?
<--- Score

78. What are the potential basics of Risk Committee fraud?
<--- Score

79. What trouble can you get into?
<--- Score

80. In a project to restructure Risk Committee outcomes, which stakeholders would you involve?
<--- Score

81. What is the kind of project structure that would be appropriate for your Risk Committee project, should it be formal and complex, or can it be less formal and relatively simple?
<--- Score

82. Can you maintain your growth without detracting from the factors that have contributed to your success?
<--- Score

83. What are your most important goals for the strategic Risk Committee objectives?
<--- Score

84. Do you feel that more should be done in the Risk Committee area?
<--- Score

85. How long will it take to change?
<--- Score

86. Ask yourself: how would you do this work if you only had one staff member to do it?
<--- Score

87. Are you / should you be revolutionary or evolutionary?
<--- Score

88. What are the challenges?
<--- Score

89. How do you go about securing Risk Committee?
<--- Score

90. What are the rules and assumptions your industry operates under? What if the opposite were true?
<--- Score

91. How do you ensure that implementations of Risk Committee products are done in a way that ensures safety?
<--- Score

92. Where can you break convention?
<--- Score

93. If you had to rebuild your organization without any traditional competitive advantages (i.e., no killer technology, promising research, innovative product/ service delivery model, etcetera), how would your people have to approach their work and collaborate together in order to create the necessary conditions for success?
<--- Score

94. How do you transition from the baseline to the target?
<--- Score

95. Whom among your colleagues do you trust, and for what?
<--- Score

96. What Risk Committee modifications can you make work for you?
<--- Score

97. How do you deal with Risk Committee changes?
<--- Score

98. What is your Risk Committee strategy?
<--- Score

99. What is an unauthorized commitment?
<--- Score

100. How do customers see your organization?
<--- Score

101. Are you maintaining a past–present–future perspective throughout the Risk Committee discussion?
<--- Score

102. Who is on the team?
<--- Score

103. Who else should you help?
<--- Score

104. What Risk Committee skills are most important?
<--- Score

105. Who are the key stakeholders?
<--- Score

106. What are specific Risk Committee rules to follow?
<--- Score

107. How are you doing compared to your industry?
<--- Score

108. If you were responsible for initiating and implementing major changes in your organization, what steps might you take to ensure acceptance of

those changes?
<--- Score

109. Who is responsible for errors?
<--- Score

110. How is implementation research currently incorporated into each of your goals?
<--- Score

111. What is the funding source for this project?
<--- Score

112. What are the key enablers to make this Risk Committee move?
<--- Score

113. Who is the main stakeholder, with ultimate responsibility for driving Risk Committee forward?
<--- Score

114. Who do we want your customers to become?
<--- Score

115. How will you motivate the stakeholders with the least vested interest?
<--- Score

116. How do you engage the workforce, in addition to satisfying them?
<--- Score

117. Will there be any necessary staff changes (redundancies or new hires)?
<--- Score

118. How do you track customer value, profitability or financial return, organizational success, and sustainability?
<--- Score

119. What is your question? Why?
<--- Score

120. What are internal and external Risk Committee relations?
<--- Score

121. Do you think Risk Committee accomplishes the goals you expect it to accomplish?
<--- Score

122. What is the overall talent health of your organization as a whole at senior levels, and for each organization reporting to a member of the Senior Leadership Team?
<--- Score

123. What are the long-term Risk Committee goals?
<--- Score

124. What was the last experiment you ran?
<--- Score

125. To whom do you add value?
<--- Score

126. Is a Risk Committee team work effort in place?
<--- Score

127. How do you lead with Risk Committee in mind?
<--- Score

128. What information is critical to your organization that your executives are ignoring?
<--- Score

129. What does your signature ensure?
<--- Score

130. What would have to be true for the option on the table to be the best possible choice?
<--- Score

131. What counts that you are not counting?
<--- Score

132. What is the source of the strategies for Risk Committee strengthening and reform?
<--- Score

133. How important is Risk Committee to the user organizations mission?
<--- Score

134. What will be the consequences to the stakeholder (financial, reputation etc) if Risk Committee does not go ahead or fails to deliver the objectives?
<--- Score

135. Which Risk Committee goals are the most important?
<--- Score

136. What are current Risk Committee paradigms?
<--- Score

137. What new services of functionality will be implemented next with Risk Committee ?
<--- Score

138. What are your personal philosophies regarding Risk Committee and how do they influence your work?
<--- Score

139. How do you maintain Risk Committee's Integrity?
<--- Score

140. How do you provide a safe environment -physically and emotionally?
<--- Score

141. Who is responsible for Risk Committee?
<--- Score

142. What role does communication play in the success or failure of a Risk Committee project?
<--- Score

143. How will you ensure you get what you expected?
<--- Score

144. What stupid rule would you most like to kill?
<--- Score

145. How do you proactively clarify deliverables and Risk Committee quality expectations?
<--- Score

146. What must you excel at?
<--- Score

147. How will you know that the Risk Committee project has been successful?
<--- Score

148. What knowledge, skills and characteristics mark a good Risk Committee project manager?
<--- Score

149. Why not do Risk Committee?
<--- Score

150. How do you accomplish your long range Risk Committee goals?
<--- Score

151. If you find that you havent accomplished one of the goals for one of the steps of the Risk Committee strategy, what will you do to fix it?
<--- Score

152. Who is responsible for ensuring appropriate resources (time, people and money) are allocated to Risk Committee?
<--- Score

153. What management system can you use to leverage the Risk Committee experience, ideas, and concerns of the people closest to the work to be done?
<--- Score

154. Why will customers want to buy your organizations products/services?
<--- Score

155. What are the barriers to increased Risk

Committee production?
<--- Score

156. Do you have past Risk Committee successes?
<--- Score

157. What business benefits will Risk Committee goals deliver if achieved?
<--- Score

158. Is there any reason to believe the opposite of my current belief?
<--- Score

159. What are the business goals Risk Committee is aiming to achieve?
<--- Score

160. How do you listen to customers to obtain actionable information?
<--- Score

161. Whose voice (department, ethnic group, women, older workers, etc) might you have missed hearing from in your company, and how might you amplify this voice to create positive momentum for your business?
<--- Score

Add up total points for this section:
_ _ _ _ _ = Total points for this section

Divided by: _ _ _ _ _ _ (number of statements answered) = _ _ _ _ _ _
Average score for this section

Transfer your score to the Risk
Committee Index at the beginning of the
Self-Assessment.

Risk Committee and Managing Projects, Criteria for Project Managers:

1.0 Initiating Process Group: Risk Committee

1. Were resources available as planned?

2. Where must it be done?

3. If action is called for, what form should it take?

4. Are the Risk Committee project team and stakeholders meeting regularly and using a meeting agenda and taking notes to accurately document what is being covered and what happened in the weekly meetings?

5. How well did the chosen processes fit the needs of the Risk Committee project?

6. What is the NEXT thing to do?

7. What are the constraints?

8. For technology Risk Committee projects only: Are all production support stakeholders (Business unit, technical support, & user) prepared for implementation with appropriate contingency plans?

9. Realistic - are the desired results expressed in a way that the team will be motivated and believe that the required level of involvement will be obtained?

10. What are the pressing issues of the hour?

11. What is the stake of others in your Risk Committee project?

12. Measurable - are the targets measurable?

13. What technical work to do in each phase?

14. The Risk Committee project managers have maximum authority in which type of organization?

15. Are you certain deliverables are properly completed and meet quality standards?

16. What were things that you need to improve?

17. Who is involved in each phase?

18. What communication items need improvement?

19. What business situation is being addressed?

1.1 Project Charter: Risk Committee

20. How much?

21. What is the most common tool for helping define the detail?

22. Are you building in-house ?

23. Fit with other Products Compliments – Cannibalizes?

24. What changes can you make to improve?

25. How are Risk Committee projects different from operations?

26. Are there special technology requirements?

27. What is the business need?

28. Who manages integration?

29. Who are the stakeholders?

30. Is time of the essence?

31. Why the improvements?

32. What ideas do you have for initial tests of change (PDSA cycles)?

33. Customer: who are you doing the Risk Committee project for?

34. Market – identify products market, including whether it is outside of the objective: what is the purpose of the program or Risk Committee project?

35. What date will the task finish?

36. Risk Committee project deliverables: what is the Risk Committee project going to produce?

37. What material?

38. Who is the sponsor?

39. Major high-level milestone targets: what events measure progress?

1.2 Stakeholder Register: Risk Committee

40. Who is managing stakeholder engagement?

41. What & Why?

42. What is the power of the stakeholder?

43. How will reports be created?

44. Is your organization ready for change?

45. What opportunities exist to provide communications?

46. What are the major Risk Committee project milestones requiring communications or providing communications opportunities?

47. Who wants to talk about Security?

48. How should employers make voices heard?

49. How much influence do they have on the Risk Committee project?

50. How big is the gap?

1.3 Stakeholder Analysis Matrix: Risk Committee

51. Which conditions out of the control of the management are crucial for the achievement of the immediate objective?

52. What can the stakeholder prevent from happening?

53. Processes, systems, it, communications?

54. Sustainable financial backing?

55. Timescales, deadlines and pressures?

56. Who is directly responsible for decisions on issues important to the Risk Committee project?

57. What are innovative aspects of your organization?

58. Vulnerable groups; who are the vulnerable groups that might be affected by the Risk Committee project?

59. What is your organizations competitors doing?

60. Partnerships, agencies, distribution?

61. Is there a clear description of the scope of practice of the Risk Committee projects educators?

62. Who has the power to influence the outcomes of the work?

63. How affected by the problem(s)?

64. How to measure the achievement of the Immediate Objective?

65. Economy - home, abroad?

66. What makes a person a stakeholder?

67. Innovative aspects?

68. Who influences whom?

69. What are the key services, contractual arrangements, or other relationships between stakeholder groups?

70. Could any of your organizations weaknesses seriously threaten development?

2.0 Planning Process Group: Risk Committee

71. How can you make your needs known?

72. In what way has the Risk Committee project come up with innovative measures for problem-solving?

73. What will you do?

74. Why do it Risk Committee projects fail?

75. What factors are contributing to progress or delay in the achievement of products and results?

76. What good practices or successful experiences or transferable examples have been identified?

77. Is your organization showing technical capacity and leadership commitment to keep working with the Risk Committee project and to repeat it?

78. If you are late, will anybody notice?

79. Contingency planning. if a risk event occurs, what will you do?

80. How should needs be met?

81. Risk Committee project assessment; why did you do this Risk Committee project?

82. What will you do to minimize the impact should a

risk event occur?

83. To what extent do the intervention objectives and strategies of the Risk Committee project respond to your organizations plans?

84. Did you read it correctly?

85. Explanation: is what the Risk Committee project intents to solve a hard question?

86. Have more efficient (sensitive) and appropriate measures been adopted to respond to the political and socio-cultural problems identified?

87. Is the Risk Committee project making progress in helping to achieve the set results?

88. What type of estimation method are you using?

89. Does the program have follow-up mechanisms (to verify the quality of the products, punctuality of delivery, etc.) to measure progress in the achievement of the envisaged results?

90. To what extent have public/private national resources and/or counterparts been mobilized to contribute to the programs objective and produce results and impacts?

2.1 Project Management Plan: Risk Committee

91. When is a Risk Committee project management plan created?

92. Why do you manage integration?

93. Do the proposed changes from the Risk Committee project include any significant risks to safety?

94. What are the assumptions?

95. How do you manage integration?

96. What went wrong?

97. Where does all this information come from?

98. Are cost risk analysis methods applied to develop contingencies for the estimated total Risk Committee project costs?

99. What did not work so well?

100. Did the planning effort collaborate to develop solutions that integrate expertise, policies, programs, and Risk Committee projects across entities?

101. How do you organize the costs in the Risk Committee project management plan?

102. Do there need to be organizational changes?

103. Was the peer (technical) review of the cost estimates duly coordinated with the cost estimate center of expertise and addressed in the review documentation and certification?

104. Is mitigation authorized or recommended?

105. Is the budget realistic?

106. Are there any client staffing expectations?

107. Is the engineering content at a feasibility level-of-detail, and is it sufficiently complete, to provide an adequate basis for the baseline cost estimate?

108. Has the selected plan been formulated using cost effectiveness and incremental analysis techniques?

109. What are the training needs?

2.2 Scope Management Plan: Risk Committee

110. Have the key elements of a coherent Risk Committee project management strategy been established?

111. Are all key components of a Quality Assurance Plan present?

112. Is there an onboarding process in place?

113. How relevant is this attribute to this Risk Committee project or audit?

114. Product – what are you trying to accomplish and how will you know when you are finished?

115. What strengths do you have?

116. Can each item be appropriately scheduled?

117. Will the Risk Committee project deliverables become accepted in writing?

118. Are the proposed Risk Committee project purposes different than the previously authorized Risk Committee project?

119. Has a Risk Committee project Communications Plan been developed?

120. How much money have you spent?

121. Are cause and effect determined for risks when they occur?

122. Why is a scope management plan important?

123. How are you planning to maintain the scope baseline and how will you manage scope changes?

124. Have stakeholder accountabilities & responsibilities been clearly defined?

125. Deliverables -are the deliverables tangible and verifiable?

126. For which criterion is it tolerable not to meet the original parameters?

127. Does the implementation plan have an appropriate division of responsibilities?

128. Is quality monitored from the perspective of the customers needs and expectations?

2.3 Requirements Management Plan: Risk Committee

129. Will you use an assessment of the Risk Committee project environment as a tool to discover risk to the requirements process?

130. What cost metrics will be used?

131. Did you provide clear and concise specifications?

132. How will you communicate scheduled tasks to other team members?

133. Will you perform a Requirements Risk assessment and develop a plan to deal with risks?

134. How will the information be distributed?

135. Do you really need to write this document at all?

136. Are all the stakeholders ready for the transition into the user community?

137. Did you get proper approvals?

138. How knowledgeable is the primary Stakeholder(s) in the proposed application area?

139. Who will initially review the Risk Committee project work or products to ensure it meets the applicable acceptance criteria?

140. What is the earliest finish date for this Risk Committee project if it is scheduled to start on ...?

141. Is it new or replacing an existing business system or process?

142. What information regarding the Risk Committee project requirements will be reported?

143. Controlling Risk Committee project requirements involves monitoring the status of the Risk Committee project requirements and managing changes to the requirements. Who is responsible for monitoring and tracking the Risk Committee project requirements?

144. Will you use tracing to help understand the impact of a change in requirements?

145. How will bidders price evaluations be done, by deliverables, phases, or in a big bang?

146. Do you understand the role that each stakeholder will play in the requirements process?

147. Who has the authority to reject Risk Committee project requirements?

148. Is there formal agreement on who has authority to request a change in requirements?

2.4 Requirements Documentation: Risk Committee

149. What will be the integration problems?

150. What is your Elevator Speech?

151. Basic work/business process; high-level, what is being touched?

152. Completeness. are all functions required by the customer included?

153. Verifiability. can the requirements be checked?

154. Consistency. are there any requirements conflicts?

155. Who is involved?

156. Are there legal issues?

157. What images does it conjure?

158. Is new technology needed?

159. How can you document system requirements?

160. What is the risk associated with the technology?

161. How will requirements be documented and who signs off on them?

162. Are all functions required by the customer included?

163. Where are business rules being captured?

164. Can the requirement be changed without a large impact on other requirements?

165. What kind of entity is a problem ?

166. What are current process problems?

167. Where do system and software requirements come from, what are sources?

168. Where do you define what is a customer, what are the attributes of customer?

2.5 Requirements Traceability Matrix: Risk Committee

169. Will you use a Requirements Traceability Matrix?

170. How do you manage scope?

171. Do you have a clear understanding of all subcontracts in place?

172. Describe the process for approving requirements so they can be added to the traceability matrix and Risk Committee project work can be performed. Will the Risk Committee project requirements become approved in writing?

173. Why use a WBS?

174. What is the WBS?

175. Is there a requirements traceability process in place?

176. How will it affect the stakeholders personally in career?

177. What percentage of Risk Committee projects are producing traceability matrices between requirements and other work products?

178. How small is small enough?

179. Why do you manage scope?

180. What are the chronologies, contingencies, consequences, criteria?

2.6 Project Scope Statement: Risk Committee

181. Is there a process (test plans, inspections, reviews) defined for verifying outputs for each task?

182. Is an issue management process documented and filed?

183. Has the format for tracking and monitoring schedules and costs been defined?

184. Will an issue form be in use?

185. Is the Risk Committee project sponsor function identified and defined?

186. Will the qa related information be reported regularly as part of the status reporting mechanisms?

187. Will the Risk Committee project risks be managed according to the Risk Committee projects risk management process?

188. Is there a Quality Assurance Plan documented and filed?

189. Have you been able to easily identify success criteria and create objective measurements for each of the Risk Committee project scopes goal statements?

190. What are the defined meeting materials?

191. Is the plan under configuration management?

192. Is your organization structure appropriate for the Risk Committee projects size and complexity?

193. Why do you need to manage scope?

194. What should you drop in order to add something new?

195. If you were to write a list of what should not be included in the scope statement, what are the things that you would recommend be described as out-of-scope?

196. Is there a Change Management Board?

197. What process would you recommend for creating the Risk Committee project scope statement?

198. How often do you estimate that the scope might change, and why?

199. Is the Risk Committee project manager qualified and experienced in Risk Committee project management?

2.7 Assumption and Constraint Log: Risk Committee

200. What is positive about the current process?

201. Is there adequate stakeholder participation for the vetting of requirements definition, changes and management?

202. Was the document/deliverable developed per the appropriate or required standards (for example, Institute of Electrical and Electronics Engineers standards)?

203. Are requirements management tracking tools and procedures in place?

204. Are processes for release management of new development from coding and unit testing, to integration testing, to training, and production defined and followed?

205. What does an audit system look like?

206. Have all necessary approvals been obtained?

207. Is the definition of the Risk Committee project scope clear; what needs to be accomplished?

208. No superfluous information or marketing narrative?

209. Are there processes defining how software will

be developed including development methods, overall timeline for development, software product standards, and traceability?

210. Have Risk Committee project management standards and procedures been established and documented?

211. Is the amount of effort justified by the anticipated value of forming a new process?

212. How are new requirements or changes to requirements identified?

213. What do you log?

214. What would you gain if you spent time working to improve this process?

215. Does a documented Risk Committee project organizational policy & plan (i.e. governance model) exist?

216. Is there a Steering Committee in place?

217. Were the system requirements formally reviewed prior to initiating the design phase?

218. Are formal code reviews conducted?

219. Is this model reasonable?

2.8 Work Breakdown Structure: Risk Committee

220. How will you and your Risk Committee project team define the Risk Committee projects scope and work breakdown structure?

221. When does it have to be done?

222. Where does it take place?

223. When do you stop?

224. Is it a change in scope?

225. Who has to do it?

226. What has to be done?

227. How many levels?

228. Is it still viable?

229. When would you develop a Work Breakdown Structure?

230. Is the work breakdown structure (wbs) defined and is the scope of the Risk Committee project clear with assigned deliverable owners?

231. How far down?

232. How big is a work-package?

233. What is the probability that the Risk Committee project duration will exceed xx weeks?

234. What is the probability of completing the Risk Committee project in less that xx days?

235. Why is it useful?

2.9 WBS Dictionary: Risk Committee

236. Do the lines of authority for incurring indirect costs correspond to the lines of responsibility for management control of the same components of costs?

237. Are the contractors estimates of costs at completion reconcilable with cost data reported to us?

238. Does the contractors system provide for accurate cost accumulation and assignment to control accounts in a manner consistent with the budgets using recognized acceptable costing techniques?

239. Does the contractor require sufficient detailed planning of control accounts to constrain the application of budget initially allocated for future effort to current effort?

240. Are overhead cost budgets established for each organization which has authority to incur overhead costs?

241. Does the contractors system provide unit costs, equivalent unit or lot costs in terms of labor, material, other direct, and indirect costs?

242. Identify and isolate causes of favorable and unfavorable cost and schedule variances?

243. What are you counting on?

244. Are all affected work authorizations, budgeting, and scheduling documents amended to properly reflect the effects of authorized changes?

245. Authorization to proceed with all authorized work?

246. Does the contractors system description or procedures require that the performance measurement baseline plus management reserve equal the contract budget base?

247. What is the end result of a work package?

248. Identify potential or actual budget-based and time-based schedule variances?

249. Wbs elements contractually specified for reporting of status to you (lowest level only)?

250. Are records maintained to show full accountability for all material purchased for the contract, including the residual inventory?

251. Changes in the overhead pool and/or organization structures?

252. Contractor financial periods; for example, annual?

253. Are control accounts opened and closed based on the start and completion of work contained therein?

254. Are there procedures for monitoring action items and corrective actions to the point of resolution and

are corresponding procedures being followed?

2.10 Schedule Management Plan: Risk Committee

255. Quality assurance overheads?

256. Are software metrics formally captured, analyzed and used as a basis for other Risk Committee project estimates?

257. Are tasks tracked by hours?

258. Is the critical path valid?

259. Are schedule performance measures defined including pre-set triggers for specific actions?

260. Have all involved Risk Committee project stakeholders and work groups committed to the Risk Committee project?

261. Are all vendor contracts closed out?

262. Who is responsible for estimating the activity resources?

263. What is the estimated time to complete the Risk Committee project if status quo is maintained?

264. Is an industry recognized mechanized support tool(s) being used for Risk Committee project scheduling & tracking?

265. Are the people assigned to the Risk Committee

project sufficiently qualified?

266. Does the resource management plan include a personnel development plan?

267. Is the plan consistent with industry best practices?

268. Are adequate resources provided for the quality assurance function?

269. Were the budget estimates reasonable?

270. Is it standard practice to formally commit stakeholders to the Risk Committee project via agreements?

271. Does the time Risk Committee projection include an amount for contingencies (time reserves)?

2.11 Activity List: Risk Committee

272. When will the work be performed?

273. What is the probability the Risk Committee project can be completed in xx weeks?

274. What is your organizations history in doing similar activities?

275. How difficult will it be to do specific activities on this Risk Committee project?

276. What is the LF and LS for each activity?

277. Are the required resources available or need to be acquired?

278. For other activities, how much delay can be tolerated?

279. When do the individual activities need to start and finish?

280. In what sequence?

281. Can you determine the activity that must finish, before this activity can start?

282. How will it be performed?

283. What went right?

284. How can the Risk Committee project be

displayed graphically to better visualize the activities?

285. What is the total time required to complete the Risk Committee project if no delays occur?

286. How much slack is available in the Risk Committee project?

287. Who will perform the work?

288. Is there anything planned that does not need to be here?

289. Is infrastructure setup part of your Risk Committee project?

290. How detailed should a Risk Committee project get?

2.12 Activity Attributes: Risk Committee

291. How difficult will it be to do specific activities on this Risk Committee project?

292. Is there a trend during the year?

293. What conclusions/generalizations can you draw from this?

294. How difficult will it be to complete specific activities on this Risk Committee project?

295. Were there other ways you could have organized the data to achieve similar results?

296. Does your organization of the data change its meaning?

297. What is missing?

298. Activity: fair or not fair?

299. Where else does it apply?

300. Resources to accomplish the work?

301. Have constraints been applied to the start and finish milestones for the phases?

302. Why?

303. What is the general pattern here?

304. Which method produces the more accurate cost assignment?

305. What activity do you think you should spend the most time on?

306. Resource is assigned to?

307. Can more resources be added?

2.13 Milestone List: Risk Committee

308. Global influences?

309. What background experience, skills, and strengths does the team bring to your organization?

310. How late can the activity start?

311. Which path is the critical path?

312. Calculate how long can activity be delayed?

313. How late can each activity be finished and started?

314. Information and research?

315. Environmental effects?

316. Continuity, supply chain robustness?

317. Competitive advantages?

318. Can you derive how soon can the whole Risk Committee project finish?

319. Insurmountable weaknesses?

320. Identify critical paths (one or more) and which activities are on the critical path?

321. Milestone pages should display the UserID of the person who added the milestone. Does a report or

query exist that provides this audit information?

322. Describe the industry you are in and the market growth opportunities. What is the market for your technology, product or service?

323. Marketing - reach, distribution, awareness?

324. Describe your organizations strengths and core competencies. What factors will make your organization succeed?

325. What are your competitors vulnerabilities?

2.14 Network Diagram: Risk Committee

326. If a current contract exists, can you provide the vendor name, contract start, and contract expiration date?

327. Are the required resources available?

328. What is the completion time?

329. Are you on time?

330. Are the gantt chart and/or network diagram updated periodically and used to assess the overall Risk Committee project timetable?

331. Will crashing x weeks return more in benefits than it costs?

332. What are the Major Administrative Issues?

333. What are the tools?

334. Where do schedules come from?

335. Exercise: what is the probability that the Risk Committee project duration will exceed xx weeks?

336. What job or jobs precede it?

337. What job or jobs could run concurrently?

338. What are the Key Success Factors?

339. How confident can you be in your milestone dates and the delivery date?

340. What activities must follow this activity?

341. If x is long, what would be the completion time if you break x into two parallel parts of y weeks and z weeks?

342. How difficult will it be to do specific activities on this Risk Committee project?

343. What is the lowest cost to complete this Risk Committee project in xx weeks?

344. What job or jobs follow it?

2.15 Activity Resource Requirements: Risk Committee

345. Do you use tools like decomposition and rolling-wave planning to produce the activity list and other outputs?

346. Which logical relationship does the PDM use most often?

347. Time for overtime?

348. Other support in specific areas?

349. What are constraints that you might find during the Human Resource Planning process?

350. Why do you do that?

351. Anything else?

352. When does monitoring begin?

353. How do you manage time?

354. How do you handle petty cash?

355. What is the Work Plan Standard?

356. Are there unresolved issues that need to be addressed?

357. Organizational Applicability?

358. How many signatures do you require on a check and does this match what is in your policy and procedures?

2.16 Resource Breakdown Structure: Risk Committee

359. How difficult will it be to do specific activities on this Risk Committee project?

360. What are the requirements for resource data?

361. What is the difference between % Complete and % work?

362. Who is allowed to perform which functions?

363. What is the purpose of assigning and documenting responsibility?

364. What defines a successful Risk Committee project?

365. How can this help you with team building?

366. Who needs what information?

367. Why do you do it?

368. Which resources should be in the resource pool?

369. How should the information be delivered?

370. Who delivers the information?

371. Why time management?

372. What is the number one predictor of a groups productivity?

373. Why is this important?

374. What defines a successful Risk Committee project?

2.17 Activity Duration Estimates: Risk Committee

375. Is a formal written notice that the contract is complete provided to the seller?

376. Total slack can be calculated by which equations?

377. What do you think about the WBSs for them?

378. Which types of reports would help provide summary information to senior management?

379. Are operational definitions created to identify quality measurement criteria for specific activities?

380. What are the main types of contracts if you do decide to outsource?

381. Which tips for taking the PMP exam do you think would be most helpful for you?

382. Is the work performed reviewed against contractual objectives?

383. Under corresponding circumstances what would be the best thing to do?

384. After how many days will the lease cost be the same as the purchase cost for the equipment?

385. How do functionality, system outputs, performance, reliability, and maintainability

requirements affect quality planning?

386. Will it help in finding or retaining employees?

387. What Risk Committee project was the first to use modern Risk Committee project management?

388. Do your results resemble a normal distribution?

389. What are the advantages and disadvantages of PERT?

390. What does it mean to take a systems view of a Risk Committee project?

391. Do checklists exist that list frequently performed activities?

392. How does a Risk Committee project life cycle differ from a product life cycle?

2.18 Duration Estimating Worksheet: Risk Committee

393. Define the work as completely as possible. What work will be included in the Risk Committee project?

394. Does the Risk Committee project provide innovative ways for stakeholders to overcome obstacles or deliver better outcomes?

395. Is the Risk Committee project responsive to community need?

396. Why estimate time and cost?

397. What info is needed?

398. Why estimate costs?

399. Small or large Risk Committee project?

400. Is a construction detail attached (to aid in explanation)?

401. What questions do you have?

402. What is an Average Risk Committee project?

403. What work will be included in the Risk Committee project?

404. Do any colleagues have experience with your organization and/or RFPs?

405. What are the critical bottleneck activities?

406. What is next?

407. Is this operation cost effective?

408. Will the Risk Committee project collaborate with the local community and leverage resources?

409. When does your organization expect to be able to complete it?

410. When, then?

2.19 Project Schedule: Risk Committee

411. How can you shorten the schedule?

412. How do you know that youhave done this right?

413. Is infrastructure setup part of your Risk Committee project?

414. It allows the Risk Committee project to be delivered on schedule. How Do you Use Schedules?

415. Why is this particularly bad?

416. Does the condition or event threaten the Risk Committee projects objectives in any ways?

417. Are quality inspections and review activities listed in the Risk Committee project schedule(s)?

418. Should you include sub-activities?

419. Verify that the update is accurate. Are all remaining durations correct?

420. Did the final product meet or exceed user expectations?

421. Are activities connected because logic dictates the order in which others occur?

422. How detailed should a Risk Committee project

get?

423. How can you minimize or control changes to Risk Committee project schedules?

424. How do you manage Risk Committee project Risk?

425. Was the Risk Committee project schedule reviewed by all stakeholders and formally accepted?

426. Month Risk Committee project take?

427. Is the structure for tracking the Risk Committee project schedule well defined and assigned to a specific individual?

2.20 Cost Management Plan: Risk Committee

428. What is cost and Risk Committee project cost management?

429. Time management – how will the schedule impact of changes be estimated and approved?

430. Are all payments made according to the contract(s)?

431. Risk rating?

432. Are Risk Committee project team members involved in detailed estimating and scheduling?

433. Are parking lot items captured?

434. Does the business case include how the Risk Committee project aligns with your organizations strategic goals & objectives?

435. Do Risk Committee project managers participating in the Risk Committee project know the Risk Committee projects true status first hand?

436. Planning and scheduling responsibilities – How will the responsibilities for planning and scheduling be allocated?

437. For cost control purposes?

438. Cost estimate preparation – What cost estimates will be prepared during the Risk Committee project phases?

439. What is Risk Committee project cost management?

440. Is your organization certified as a supplier, wholesaler and/or regular dealer?

441. What will be the split of responsibilities of progress measurement and controls among the owner, contractor, subcontractors, and vendors?

442. Does the Risk Committee project have a formal Risk Committee project Charter?

443. Are vendor invoices audited for accuracy before payment?

444. Forecasts – how will the time and resources needed to complete the Risk Committee project be forecast?

445. Has a quality assurance plan been developed for the Risk Committee project?

2.21 Activity Cost Estimates: Risk Committee

446. Can you change your activities?

447. Can you delete activities or make them inactive?

448. Does the activity use a common approach or business function to deliver its results?

449. What happens if you cannot produce the documentation for the single audit?

450. Which contract type places the most risk on the seller?

451. What were things that you did well, and could improve, and how?

452. Is costing method consistent with study goals?

453. What areas does the group agree are the biggest success on the Risk Committee project?

454. How difficult will it be to do specific tasks on the Risk Committee project?

455. What are you looking for?

456. Will you need to provide essential services information about activities?

457. If you are asked to lower your estimate because

the price is too high, what are your options?

458. What makes a good activity description?

459. Were escalated issues resolved promptly?

460. Did the Risk Committee project team have the right skills?

461. Would you hire them again?

462. Specific - is the objective clear in terms of what, how, when, and where the situation will be changed?

2.22 Cost Estimating Worksheet: Risk Committee

463. What will others want?

464. What additional Risk Committee project(s) could be initiated as a result of this Risk Committee project?

465. Identify the timeframe necessary to monitor progress and collect data to determine how the selected measure has changed?

466. Will the Risk Committee project collaborate with the local community and leverage resources?

467. What happens to any remaining funds not used?

468. Does the Risk Committee project provide innovative ways for stakeholders to overcome obstacles or deliver better outcomes?

469. Is the Risk Committee project responsive to community need?

470. What can be included?

471. Value pocket identification & quantification what are value pockets?

472. What is the estimated labor cost today based upon this information?

473. Can a trend be established from historical

performance data on the selected measure and are the criteria for using trend analysis or forecasting methods met?

474. How will the results be shared and to whom?

475. Who is best positioned to know and assist in identifying corresponding factors?

476. What costs are to be estimated?

477. What is the purpose of estimating?

478. Is it feasible to establish a control group arrangement?

479. Ask: are others positioned to know, are others credible, and will others cooperate?

2.23 Cost Baseline: Risk Committee

480. What deliverables come first?

481. Has operations management formally accepted responsibility for operating and maintaining the product(s) or service(s) delivered by the Risk Committee project?

482. What do you want to measure ?

483. What is your organizations history in doing similar tasks?

484. How will cost estimates be used?

485. Has training and knowledge transfer of the operations organization been completed?

486. Review your risk triggers -have your risks changed?

487. What would the life cycle costs be?

488. What is the reality?

489. Escalation criteria met?

490. Where do changes come from?

491. Definition of done can be traced back to the definitions of what are you providing to the customer in terms of deliverables?

492. What weaknesses do you have?

493. Have the resources used by the Risk Committee project been reassigned to other units or Risk Committee projects?

494. What can go wrong?

495. Does a process exist for establishing a cost baseline to measure Risk Committee project performance?

496. How likely is it to go wrong?

497. What is cost and Risk Committee project cost management?

2.24 Quality Management Plan: Risk Committee

498. How many Risk Committee project staff does this specific process affect?

499. How are data handled when a test is not run per specification?

500. After observing execution of process, is it in compliance with the documented Plan?

501. Sampling part of task?

502. How are changes to procedures made?

503. How are changes recorded?

504. How do senior leaders create your organizational focus on customers and other stakeholders?

505. Are there processes in place to ensure internal consistency between the source code components?

506. Have all involved stakeholders and work groups committed to the Risk Committee project?

507. Who gets results of work?

508. Do trained quality assurance auditors conduct the audits as defined in the Quality Management Plan and scheduled by the Risk Committee project manager?

509. What are your key performance measures/ indicators for tracking progress relative to your action plans?

510. How does your organization establish and maintain customer relationships?

511. Does a prospective decision remain the same regardless of what the data show is?

512. Does the program conduct field testing?

513. Who is responsible?

514. How does your organization design processes to ensure others meet customer and others requirements?

515. How does your organization use comparative data and information to improve organizational performance?

516. How is staff trained in procedures?

2.25 Quality Metrics: Risk Committee

517. What metrics do you measure?

518. What about still open problems?

519. There are many reasons to shore up quality-related metrics, and what metrics are important?

520. How do you calculate such metrics?

521. What documentation is required?

522. Are quality metrics defined?

523. How are requirements conflicts resolved?

524. What forces exist that would cause them to change?

525. How is it being measured?

526. Has it met internal or external standards?

527. What happens if you get an abnormal result?

528. Are interface issues coordinated?

529. Is material complete (and does it meet the standards)?

530. Where is quality now?

531. Is there a set of procedures to capture, analyze

and act on quality metrics?

532. How effective are your security tests?

533. Has risk analysis been adequately reviewed?

534. What group is empowered to define quality requirements?

535. What is the CMS Benchmark?

2.26 Process Improvement Plan: Risk Committee

536. Does your process ensure quality?

537. What lessons have you learned so far?

538. Are you following the quality standards?

539. Why quality management?

540. Where are you now?

541. Management commitment at all levels?

542. What personnel are the sponsors for that initiative?

543. What personnel are the change agents for your initiative?

544. Are there forms and procedures to collect and record the data?

545. Everyone agrees on what process improvement is, right?

546. How do you manage quality?

547. What personnel are the coaches for your initiative?

548. What makes people good SPI coaches?

549. Why do you want to achieve the goal?

550. Where do you want to be?

551. Are you making progress on your improvement plan?

552. Are you meeting the quality standards?

553. Have the frequency of collection and the points in the process where measurements will be made been determined?

554. Modeling current processes is great, and will you ever see a return on that investment?

2.27 Responsibility Assignment Matrix: Risk Committee

555. Will too many Communicating responsibilities tangle the Risk Committee project in unnecessary communications?

556. The anticipated business volume?

557. Is work progressively subdivided into detailed work packages as requirements are defined?

558. What expertise is available in your department?

559. Not any rs, as, or cs: if an identified role is only informed, should others be eliminated from the matrix?

560. Does the scheduling system identify in a timely manner the status of work?

561. Cwbs elements to be subcontracted, with identification of subcontractors?

562. Do work packages consist of discrete tasks which are adequately described?

563. Actual cost of work performed?

564. Most people let you know when others re too busy, and are others really too busy?

565. Are significant decision points, constraints, and

interfaces identified as key milestones?

566. If a role has only Signing-off, or only Communicating responsibility and has no Performing, Accountable, or Monitoring responsibility, is it necessary?

567. Does the Risk Committee project need to be analyzed further to uncover additional responsibilities?

568. Does each activity-deliverable have exactly one Accountable responsibility, so that accountability is clear and decisions can be made quickly?

569. Will too many Signing-off responsibilities delay the completion of the activity/deliverable?

570. What are the deliverables?

2.28 Roles and Responsibilities: Risk Committee

571. Required skills, knowledge, experience?

572. Be specific; avoid generalities. Thank you and great work alone are insufficient. What exactly do you appreciate and why?

573. How well did the Risk Committee project Team understand the expectations of specific roles and responsibilities?

574. Concern: where are you limited or have no authority, where you can not influence?

575. Is there a training program in place for stakeholders covering expectations, roles and responsibilities and any addition knowledge others need to be good stakeholders?

576. Does the team have access to and ability to use data analysis tools?

577. Are your budgets supportive of a culture of quality data?

578. Is feedback clearly communicated and non-judgmental?

579. What areas would you highlight for changes or improvements?

580. Are your policies supportive of a culture of quality data?

581. Accountabilities: what are the roles and responsibilities of individual team members?

582. Who is responsible for each task?

583. What is working well?

584. Are governance roles and responsibilities documented?

585. What specific behaviors did you observe?

586. Have you ever been a part of this team?

587. What expectations were NOT met?

2.29 Human Resource Management Plan: Risk Committee

588. Is your organization heading towards expansion, outsourcing of certain talents or making cut-backs to save money?

589. Have Risk Committee project management standards and procedures been identified / established and documented?

590. Are target dates established for each milestone deliverable?

591. Are the people assigned to the Risk Committee project sufficiently qualified?

592. Is there an on-going process in place to monitor Risk Committee project risks?

593. Are issues raised, assessed, actioned, and resolved in a timely and efficient manner?

594. Is there an issues management plan in place?

595. Is documentation created for communication with the suppliers and Vendors?

596. Account for the purpose of this Risk Committee project by describing, at a high-level, what will be done. What is this Risk Committee project aiming to achieve?

597. Is this Risk Committee project carried out in partnership with other groups/organizations?

598. Is Risk Committee project status reviewed with the steering and executive teams at appropriate intervals?

599. What is the boss?

600. Are decisions captured in a decisions log?

601. Does the business case include how the Risk Committee project aligns with your organizations strategic goals & objectives?

602. Staffing Requirements?

603. Are people motivated to meet the current and future challenges?

604. Has the scope management document been updated and distributed to help prevent scope creep?

605. Are there checklists created to determine if all quality processes are followed?

2.30 Communications Management Plan: Risk Committee

606. How often do you engage with stakeholders?

607. What communications method?

608. Who is the stakeholder?

609. Is the stakeholder role recognized by your organization?

610. Are there potential barriers between the team and the stakeholder?

611. What does the stakeholder need from the team?

612. Are there too many who have an interest in some aspect of your work?

613. What is the stakeholders level of authority?

614. What approaches do you use?

615. Are you constantly rushing from meeting to meeting?

616. Who did you turn to if you had questions?

617. Are others needed?

618. Who needs to know and how much?

619. Will messages be directly related to the release strategy or phases of the Risk Committee project?

620. Do you then often overlook a key stakeholder or stakeholder group?

621. Why manage stakeholders?

622. How will the person responsible for executing the communication item be notified?

623. What to learn?

624. Where do team members get information?

2.31 Risk Management Plan: Risk Committee

625. Where do risks appear in the business phases?

626. Are the reports useful and easy to read?

627. Are some people working on multiple Risk Committee projects?

628. Why do you want risk management?

629. How risk averse are you?

630. Is Risk Committee project scope stable?

631. What things might go wrong?

632. Is the technology to be built new to your organization?

633. Risks should be identified during which phase of Risk Committee project management life cycle?

634. Why is product liability a serious issue?

635. Do requirements demand the use of new analysis, design, or testing methods?

636. Was an original risk assessment/risk management plan completed?

637. Are Risk Committee project requirements stable?

638. Do benefits and chances of success outweigh potential damage if success is not attained?

639. Have customers been involved fully in the definition of requirements?

640. Are there risks to human health or the environment that need to be controlled or mitigated?

641. Does the Risk Committee project have the authority and ability to avoid the risk?

642. Are the participants able to keep up with the workload?

643. How do you manage Risk Committee project Risk?

644. What would you do differently?

2.32 Risk Register: Risk Committee

645. Are there any gaps in the evidence?

646. What will be done?

647. Technology risk -is the Risk Committee project technically feasible?

648. Methodology: how will risk management be performed on this Risk Committee project?

649. Cost/benefit – how much will the proposed mitigations cost and how does this cost compare with the potential cost of the risk event/situation should it occur?

650. Do you require further engagement?

651. When would you develop a risk register?

652. How could corresponding Risk affect the Risk Committee project in terms of cost and schedule?

653. How often will the Risk Management Plan and Risk Register be formally reviewed, and by whom?

654. What could prevent you delivering on the strategic program objectives and what is being done to mitigate corresponding issues?

655. Assume the risk event or situation happens, what would the impact be?

656. What risks might negatively or positively affect achieving the Risk Committee project objectives?

657. What are the assumptions and current status that support the assessment of the risk?

658. Can the likelihood and impact of failing to achieve corresponding recommendations and action plans be assessed?

659. Manageability – have mitigations to the risk been identified?

660. Budget and schedule: what are the estimated costs and schedules for performing risk-related activities?

661. When is it going to be done?

662. What evidence do you have to justify the likelihood score of the risk (audit, incident report, claim, complaints, inspection, internal review)?

663. What is the appropriate level of risk management for this Risk Committee project?

2.33 Probability and Impact Assessment: Risk Committee

664. Has something like this been done before?

665. Does the software engineering team have the right mix of skills?

666. Are tool mentors available?

667. Are the risk data timely and relevant?

668. What significant shift will occur in governmental policies, laws, and regulations pertaining to specific industries?

669. Risks should be identified during which phase of Risk Committee project management life cycle?

670. When and how will the recent breakthroughs in basic research lead to commercial products?

671. Should the risk be taken at all?

672. Why has this particular mode of contracting been chosen?

673. How would you suggest monitoring for risk transition indicators?

674. Is security a central objective?

675. How completely has the customer been

identified?

676. What action do you usually take against risks?

677. Who should be responsible for the monitoring and tracking of the indicators youhave identified?

678. How much risk do others need to take?

679. What are the likely future requirements?

680. What risks are necessary to achieve success?

681. What things are likely to change?

682. Do you have specific methods that you use for each phase of the process?

2.34 Probability and Impact Matrix: Risk Committee

683. What should be done with risks on the watch list?

684. Why do you need to manage Risk Committee project Risk?

685. What are the probable external agencies to act as Risk Committee project manager?

686. Mitigation -how can you avoid the risk?

687. What are data sources?

688. Which is an input to the risk management process?

689. Management -what contingency plans do you have if the risk becomes a reality?

690. What will be the likely political environment during the life of the Risk Committee project?

691. Is a software Risk Committee project management tool available?

692. What can possibly go wrong?

693. Can you avoid altogether some things that might go wrong?

694. How realistic is the timing of introduction?

695. Is there any sign of biased ranking?

696. What is the probability of the risk occurring?

697. While preparing your risk responses, you identify additional risks. What should you do?

698. Which is the BEST thing to do?

699. How well is the risk understood?

2.35 Risk Data Sheet: Risk Committee

700. During work activities could hazards exist?

701. What actions can be taken to eliminate or remove risk?

702. Do effective diagnostic tests exist?

703. What are you weak at and therefore need to do better?

704. What is the environment within which you operate (social trends, economic, community values, broad based participation, national directions etc.)?

705. What can you do?

706. Has a sensitivity analysis been carried out?

707. What was measured?

708. What if client refuses?

709. Risk of what?

710. What is the chance that it will happen?

711. Who has a vested interest in how you perform as your organization (our stakeholders)?

712. Are new hazards created?

713. Has the most cost-effective solution been

chosen?

714. What can happen?

715. How reliable is the data source?

716. What do you know?

717. What do people affected think about the need for, and practicality of preventive measures?

2.36 Procurement Management Plan: Risk Committee

718. Are Risk Committee project team roles and responsibilities identified and documented?

719. Are changes in deliverable commitments agreed to by all affected groups & individuals?

720. Is there a formal process for updating the Risk Committee project baseline?

721. Are internal Risk Committee project status meetings held at reasonable intervals?

722. Are quality inspections and review activities listed in the Risk Committee project schedule(s)?

723. What are things that you need to improve?

724. Is there a requirements change management processes in place?

725. Was the scope definition used in task sequencing?

726. Is stakeholder involvement adequate?

727. Has the budget been baselined?

728. Are software metrics formally captured, analyzed and used as a basis for other Risk Committee project estimates?

729. Has your organization readiness assessment been conducted?

730. Are the schedule estimates reasonable given the Risk Committee project?

731. Does the Risk Committee project team have the right skills?

732. Are trade-offs between accepting the risk and mitigating the risk identified?

733. Is the schedule updated on a periodic basis?

734. Has a provision been made to reassess Risk Committee project risks at various Risk Committee project stages?

2.37 Source Selection Criteria: Risk Committee

735. Are they compliant with all technical requirements?

736. How can the methods of publicizing the buy be tailored to yield more effective price competition?

737. What are the guiding principles for developing an evaluation report?

738. How organization are proposed quotes/prices?

739. If the costs are normalized, please account for how the normalization is conducted. Is a cost realism analysis used?

740. When should debriefings be held and how should they be scheduled?

741. How long will it take for the purchase cost to be the same as the lease cost?

742. What can not be disclosed?

743. What should be considered when developing evaluation standards?

744. What should be the contracting officers strategy?

745. What source selection software is your team using?

746. Are there any common areas of weaknesses or deficiencies in the proposals in the competitive range?

747. When must you conduct a debriefing?

748. In which phase of the acquisition process cycle does source qualifications reside?

749. Is a cost realism analysis used?

750. When is it appropriate to conduct a preproposal conference?

751. Are considerations anticipated?

752. What past performance information should be requested?

753. Are there any specific considerations that precludes offers from being selected as the awardee?

754. Do you want to wait until all offerors have been evaluated?

2.38 Stakeholder Management Plan: Risk Committee

755. Are the Risk Committee project team members located locally to the users/stakeholders?

756. Has a resource management plan been created?

757. Does the business case include how the Risk Committee project aligns with your organizations strategic goals & objectives?

758. Does the system design reflect the requirements?

759. Is the performance of the supplier to be rated and documented?

760. Are milestone deliverables effectively tracked and compared to Risk Committee project plan?

761. Has a capability assessment been conducted?

762. Does the detailed work plan match the complexity of tasks with the capabilities of personnel?

763. Are all resource assumptions documented?

764. What is meant by managing the triple constraint?

765. Has the Risk Committee project scope been baselined?

766. Does the role of the Risk Committee project

Team cease upon the delivery of the Risk Committee projects outputs?

767. Have all involved Risk Committee project stakeholders and work groups committed to the Risk Committee project?

768. What training requirements are there based upon the required skills and resources?

769. Does the Risk Committee project have a Quality Culture?

770. Can the requirements be traced to the appropriate components of the solution, as well as test scripts?

771. Are risk triggers captured?

2.39 Change Management Plan: Risk Committee

772. What new competencies will be required for the roles?

773. Is there a support model for this application and are the details available for distribution?

774. Who will be the change levers?

775. What policies and procedures need to be changed?

776. Is there a software application relevant to this deliverable?

777. What work practices will be affected?

778. What new roles are needed?

779. Has a training need analysis been carried out?

780. Do there need to be new channels developed?

781. Do you need a new organization structure?

782. What processes are in place to manage knowledge about the Risk Committee project?

783. What risks may occur upfront?

784. What type of materials/channels will be available

to leverage?

785. Will the culture embrace or reject this change?

786. How do you know the requirements you documented are the right ones?

787. Is there a need for new relationships to be built?

788. What are you trying to achieve as a result of communication?

789. Have the systems been configured and tested?

790. What is the negative impact of communicating too soon or too late?

3.0 Executing Process Group: Risk Committee

791. How could you control progress of your Risk Committee project?

792. What are deliverables of your Risk Committee project?

793. How will you know you did it?

794. Are the necessary foundations in place to ensure the sustainability of the results of the programme?

795. Do the products created live up to the necessary quality?

796. If a risk event occurs, what will you do?

797. Do Risk Committee project managers understand your organizational context for Risk Committee projects?

798. Is the schedule for the set products being met?

799. How will you avoid scope creep?

800. How can your organization use a weighted decision matrix to evaluate proposals as part of source selection?

801. What is the product of your Risk Committee project?

802. How do you enter durations, link tasks, and view critical path information?

803. Do schedule issues conflicts?

804. Were sponsors and decision makers available when needed outside regularly scheduled meetings?

805. Why should Risk Committee project managers strive to make jobs look easy?

3.1 Team Member Status Report: Risk Committee

806. The problem with Reward & Recognition Programs is that the truly deserving people all too often get left out. How can you make it practical?

807. What specific interest groups do you have in place?

808. How will resource planning be done?

809. Does your organization have the means (staff, money, contract, etc.) to produce or to acquire the product, good, or service?

810. Are the products of your organizations Risk Committee projects meeting customers objectives?

811. Does the product, good, or service already exist within your organization?

812. Is there evidence that staff is taking a more professional approach toward management of your organizations Risk Committee projects?

813. How much risk is involved?

814. How does this product, good, or service meet the needs of the Risk Committee project and your organization as a whole?

815. When a teams productivity and success depend

on collaboration and the efficient flow of information, what generally fails them?

816. How can you make it practical?

817. Are your organizations Risk Committee projects more successful over time?

818. How it is to be done?

819. Do you have an Enterprise Risk Committee project Management Office (EPMO)?

820. Are the attitudes of staff regarding Risk Committee project work improving?

821. What is to be done?

822. Will the staff do training or is that done by a third party?

823. Why is it to be done?

824. Does every department have to have a Risk Committee project Manager on staff?

3.2 Change Request: Risk Committee

825. How shall the implementation of changes be recorded?

826. What type of changes does change control take into account?

827. When do you create a change request?

828. What is the change request log?

829. Have scm procedures for noting the change, recording it, and reporting it been followed?

830. Are there requirements attributes that are strongly related to the complexity and size?

831. Who will perform the change?

832. How well do experienced software developers predict software change?

833. Will the change use memory to the extent that other functions will be not have sufficient memory to operate effectively?

834. Should a more thorough impact analysis be conducted?

835. What kind of information about the change request needs to be captured?

836. How many lines of code must be changed to

implement the change?

837. What are the requirements for urgent changes?

838. How do team members communicate with each other?

839. Describe how modifications, enhancements, defects and/or deficiencies shall be notified (e.g. Problem Reports, Change Requests etc) and managed. Detail warranty and/or maintenance periods?

840. Has the change been highlighted and documented in the CSCI?

841. Are there requirements attributes that can discriminate between high and low reliability?

842. How are changes graded and who is responsible for the rating?

843. How is quality being addressed on the Risk Committee project?

3.3 Change Log: Risk Committee

844. Is the submitted change a new change or a modification of a previously approved change?

845. How does this change affect scope?

846. Is this a mandatory replacement?

847. Is the change backward compatible without limitations?

848. When was the request approved?

849. Does the suggested change request seem to represent a necessary enhancement to the product?

850. Will the Risk Committee project fail if the change request is not executed?

851. Is the change request within Risk Committee project scope?

852. Does the suggested change request represent a desired enhancement to the products functionality?

853. When was the request submitted?

854. Do the described changes impact on the integrity or security of the system?

855. Who initiated the change request?

856. Is the requested change request a result of

changes in other Risk Committee project(s)?

857. How does this change affect the timeline of the schedule?

858. Is the change request open, closed or pending?

859. How does this relate to the standards developed for specific business processes?

3.4 Decision Log: Risk Committee

860. Behaviors; what are guidelines that the team has identified that will assist them with getting the most out of team meetings?

861. Does anything need to be adjusted?

862. Meeting purpose; why does this team meet?

863. At what point in time does loss become unacceptable?

864. What is the average size of your matters in an applicable measurement?

865. Do strategies and tactics aimed at less than full control reduce the costs of management or simply shift the cost burden?

866. What are the cost implications?

867. How do you define success?

868. Decision-making process; how will the team make decisions?

869. What is your overall strategy for quality control / quality assurance procedures?

870. How effective is maintaining the log at facilitating organizational learning?

871. Is your opponent open to a non-traditional

workflow, or will it likely challenge anything you do?

872. How does the use a Decision Support System influence the strategies/tactics or costs?

873. What makes you different or better than others companies selling the same thing?

874. Which variables make a critical difference?

875. With whom was the decision shared or considered?

876. What eDiscovery problem or issue did your organization set out to fix or make better?

877. Is everything working as expected?

878. What alternatives/risks were considered?

879. What is the line where eDiscovery ends and document review begins?

3.5 Quality Audit: Risk Committee

880. How does your organization know that its staff financial services are appropriately effective and constructive?

881. How does your organization know that its Strategic Plan is providing the best guidance for the future of your organization?

882. How does your organization know that its system for recruiting the best staff possible are appropriately effective and constructive?

883. How does your organization know that the support for its staff is appropriately effective and constructive?

884. How does your organization know that its management of its ethical responsibilities is appropriately effective and constructive?

885. How does your organization know that the review processes are effective?

886. Can your organization demonstrate exactly how and why results were achieved?

887. How do you indicate the extent to which your personnel would be expected to contribute to the work effort?

888. What does the organizarion look for in a Quality audit?

889. How does your organization know that its system for managing intellectual property issues is appropriately effective, constructive and fair?

890. Are salvageable and salvaged medical devices stored in a manner to prevent damage and/or contamination?

891. How does your organization know that its processes for managing severance are appropriately effective, constructive and fair?

892. How does your organization know that the range and quality of its accommodation, catering and transportation services are appropriately effective and constructive?

893. Do the suppliers use a formal quality system?

894. How does your organization know that its systems for meeting staff extracurricular learning support requirements are appropriately effective and constructive?

895. If your organization thinks it is doing something well, can it prove this?

896. How does your organization know that its staff are presenting original work, and properly acknowledging the work of others?

897. Does your organization have set of goals, objectives, strategies and targets that are clearly understood by the Board and staff?

898. Are the review comments incorporated?

899. Are training programs documented?

3.6 Team Directory: Risk Committee

900. Process decisions: are all start-up, turn over and close out requirements of the contract satisfied?

901. Have you decided when to celebrate the Risk Committee projects completion date?

902. Where will the product be used and/or delivered or built when appropriate?

903. Who will be the stakeholders on your next Risk Committee project?

904. How do unidentified risks impact the outcome of the Risk Committee project?

905. How will the team handle changes?

906. How and in what format should information be presented?

907. Who should receive information (all stakeholders)?

908. How will you accomplish and manage the objectives?

909. Process decisions: is work progressing on schedule and per contract requirements?

910. Who are the Team Members?

911. How does the team resolve conflicts and ensure

tasks are completed?

912. Do purchase specifications and configurations match requirements?

913. Where should the information be distributed?

914. What needs to be communicated?

915. Process decisions: are contractors adequately prosecuting the work?

916. When will you produce deliverables?

917. Process decisions: which organizational elements and which individuals will be assigned management functions?

918. Process decisions: how well was task order work performed?

3.7 Team Operating Agreement: Risk Committee

919. Communication protocols: how will the team communicate?

920. What is the anticipated procedure (recruitment, solicitation of volunteers, or assignment) for selecting team members?

921. Did you determine the technology methods that best match the messages to be communicated?

922. Are there the right people on your team?

923. Methodologies: how will key team processes be implemented, such as training, research, work deliverable production, review and approval processes, knowledge management, and meeting procedures?

924. Do you upload presentation materials in advance and test the technology?

925. Did you prepare participants for the next meeting?

926. Is compensation based on team and individual performance?

927. How will your group handle planned absences?

928. How will you divide work equitably?

929. What are the current caseload numbers in the unit?

930. How will group handle unplanned absences?

931. Do you send out the agenda and meeting materials in advance?

932. Are there more than two national cultures represented by your team?

933. Do you ask participants to close laptops and place mobile devices on silent on the table while the meeting is in progress?

934. Did you delegate tasks such as taking meeting minutes, presenting a topic and soliciting input?

935. What resources can be provided for the team in terms of equipment, space, time for training, protected time and space for meetings, and travel allowances?

936. Do you call or email participants to ensure understanding, follow-through and commitment to the meeting outcomes?

937. Do you record meetings for the already stated unable to attend?

938. Why does your organization want to participate in teaming?

3.8 Team Performance Assessment: Risk Committee

939. What makes opportunities more or less obvious?

940. Is there a particular method of data analysis that you would recommend as a means of demonstrating that method variance is not of great concern for a given dataset?

941. When a reviewer complains about method variance, what is the essence of the complaint?

942. Lack of method variance in self-reported affect and perceptions at work: Reality or artifact?

943. To what degree are the members clear on what they are individually responsible for and what they are jointly responsible for?

944. To what degree does the teams work approach provide opportunity for members to engage in open interaction?

945. To what degree are sub-teams possible or necessary?

946. Do friends perform better than acquaintances?

947. If you have criticized someones work for method variance in your role as reviewer, what was the circumstance?

948. To what degree do team members agree with the goals, relative importance, and the ways in which achievement will be measured?

949. Does more radicalness mean more perceived benefits?

950. To what degree do members articulate the goals beyond the team membership?

951. To what degree can team members vigorously define the teams purpose in considerations with others who are not part of the functioning team?

952. To what degree do members understand and articulate the same purpose without relying on ambiguous abstractions?

953. How hard did you try to make a good selection?

954. Do you give group members authority to make at least some important decisions?

955. Effects of crew composition on crew performance: Does the whole equal the sum of its parts?

956. To what degree will the team adopt a concrete, clearly understood, and agreed-upon approach that will result in achievement of the teams goals?

957. Can familiarity breed backup?

3.9 Team Member Performance Assessment: Risk Committee

958. Does the rater (supervisor) have the authority or responsibility to tell an employee that the employees performance is unsatisfactory?

959. Goals met?

960. How are training activities developed from a technical perspective?

961. How is your organizations Strategic Management System tied to performance measurement?

962. Who receives a benchmark visit?

963. What qualities does a successful Team leader possess?

964. What is a significant fact or event?

965. What is the role of the Reviewer?

966. Are any validation activities performed?

967. What are the basic principles and objectives of performance measurement and assessment?

968. To what degree are the goals realistic?

969. How should adaptive assessments be implemented?

970. What evidence supports your decision-making?

971. To what degree do team members understand one anothers roles and skills?

972. To what degree can all members engage in open and interactive considerations?

973. What types of learning are targeted (e.g., cognitive, affective, psychomotor, procedural)?

974. What resources do you need?

975. To what degree can the team measure progress against specific goals?

976. What is collaboration?

3.10 Issue Log: Risk Committee

977. In classifying stakeholders, which approach to do so are you using?

978. Are they needed?

979. Why not more evaluators?

980. Is the issue log kept in a safe place?

981. What is the status of the issue?

982. Who reported the issue?

983. Do you feel a register helps?

984. Do you prepare stakeholder engagement plans?

985. Is access to the Issue Log controlled?

986. What is a change?

987. What is the stakeholders political influence?

988. What effort will a change need?

989. Who were proponents/opponents?

990. Do you feel more overwhelmed by stakeholders?

991. Are the stakeholders getting the information they need, are they consulted, are concerns addressed?

992. What is the impact on the risks?

993. Who do you turn to if you have questions?

994. How do you manage communications?

4.0 Monitoring and Controlling Process Group: Risk Committee

995. Propriety: who needs to be involved in the evaluation to be ethical?

996. What do they need to know about the Risk Committee project?

997. In what way has the program come up with innovative measures for problem-solving?

998. How many potential communications channels exist on the Risk Committee project?

999. Have operating capacities been created and/or reinforced in partners?

1000. Use: how will they use the information?

1001. What is the expected monetary value of the Risk Committee project?

1002. Do clients benefit (change) from the services?

1003. What areas were overlooked on this Risk Committee project?

1004. How do you monitor progress?

1005. Is the program in place as intended?

1006. How well did you do?

1007. What are the goals of the program?

1008. What resources (both financial and non-financial) are available/needed?

1009. Is progress on outcomes due to your program?

1010. Purpose: toward what end is the evaluation being conducted?

1011. What departments are involved in its daily operation?

1012. Did the Risk Committee project team have enough people to execute the Risk Committee project plan?

4.1 Project Performance Report: Risk Committee

1013. To what degree are the demands of the task compatible with and converge with the mission and functions of the formal organization?

1014. What is the degree to which rules govern information exchange between individuals within your organization?

1015. To what degree does the teams work approach provide opportunity for members to engage in results-based evaluation?

1016. To what degree do the relationships of the informal organization motivate taskrelevant behavior and facilitate task completion?

1017. To what degree are the structures of the formal organization consistent with the behaviors in the informal organization?

1018. To what degree will the team ensure that all members equitably share the work essential to the success of the team?

1019. To what degree can the cognitive capacity of individuals accommodate the flow of information?

1020. To what degree do team members feel that the purpose of the team is important, if not exciting?

1021. How is the data used?

1022. What degree are the relative importance and priority of the goals clear to all team members?

1023. To what degree can the team ensure that all members are individually and jointly accountable for the teams purpose, goals, approach, and work-products?

1024. To what degree will team members, individually and collectively, commit time to help themselves and others learn and develop skills?

1025. To what degree are the demands of the task compatible with and converge with the relationships of the informal organization?

1026. To what degree do team members articulate the teams work approach?

1027. To what degree is the team cognizant of small wins to be celebrated along the way?

1028. To what degree do the goals specify concrete team work products?

4.2 Variance Analysis: Risk Committee

1029. Contemplated overhead expenditure for each period based on the best information currently is available?

1030. Are the wbs and organizational levels for application of the Risk Committee projected overhead costs identified?

1031. What is the actual cost of work performed?

1032. Favorable or unfavorable variance?

1033. Are there changes in the direct base to which overhead costs are allocated?

1034. Wbs elements contractually specified for reporting of status to your organization (lowest level only)?

1035. Can the contractor substantiate work package and planning package budgets?

1036. What is the total budget for the Risk Committee project (including estimates for authorized and unpriced work)?

1037. Are management actions taken to reduce indirect costs when there are significant adverse variances?

1038. What causes selling price variance?

1039. How does your organization measure performance?

1040. Are there changes in the overhead pool and/or organization structures?

1041. Are all authorized tasks assigned to identified organizational elements?

1042. Does the contractors system provide unit or lot costs when applicable?

1043. Why are standard cost systems used?

1044. Is there a logical explanation for any variance?

1045. What is the incurrence of actual indirect costs in excess of budgets, by element of expense?

1046. Are meaningful indicators identified for use in measuring the status of cost and schedule performance?

4.3 Earned Value Status: Risk Committee

1047. Where is evidence-based earned value in your organization reported?

1048. When is it going to finish?

1049. Earned value can be used in almost any Risk Committee project situation and in almost any Risk Committee project environment. it may be used on large Risk Committee projects, medium sized Risk Committee projects, tiny Risk Committee projects (in cut-down form), complex and simple Risk Committee projects and in any market sector. some people, of course, know all about earned value, they have used it for years - but perhaps not as effectively as they could have?

1050. Are you hitting your Risk Committee projects targets?

1051. How does this compare with other Risk Committee projects?

1052. What is the unit of forecast value?

1053. Verification is a process of ensuring that the developed system satisfies the stakeholders agreements and specifications; Are you building the product right? What do you verify?

1054. Validation is a process of ensuring that

the developed system will actually achieve the stakeholders desired outcomes; Are you building the right product? What do you validate?

1055. Where are your problem areas?

1056. If earned value management (EVM) is so good in determining the true status of a Risk Committee project and Risk Committee project its completion, why is it that hardly any one uses it in information systems related Risk Committee projects?

1057. How much is it going to cost by the finish?

4.4 Risk Audit: Risk Committee

1058. If applicable; which route/packaging option do you choose for transport of hazmat material?

1059. Where will the next scandal or adverse media involving your organization come from?

1060. Does your board meet regularly and document all decisions and actions?

1061. Do you promote education and training opportunities?

1062. Are procedures in place to ensure the security of staff and information and compliance with privacy legislation if applicable?

1063. What are the risks that could stop you from achieving your KPIs?

1064. Has an event time line been developed?

1065. Have staff received necessary training?

1066. Do you meet all obligations relating to funds secured from grants, loans and sponsors?

1067. Is there (or should there be) some impact on the process of setting materiality when the auditor more effectively identifies higher risk areas of the financial statements?

1068. Are all participants informed of safety issues?

1069. How effective are your risk controls?

1070. Are tools for analysis and design available?

1071. Does willful intent modify risk-based auditing?

1072. Are contracts reviewed before renewal?

1073. Is the process supported by tools?

1074. Do you have an understanding of insurance claims processes?

1075. How will you maximise opportunities?

4.5 Contractor Status Report: Risk Committee

1076. Who can list a Risk Committee project as organization experience, your organization or a previous employee of your organization?

1077. How long have you been using the services?

1078. What are the minimum and optimal bandwidth requirements for the proposed solution?

1079. Are there contractual transfer concerns?

1080. Describe how often regular updates are made to the proposed solution. Are corresponding regular updates included in the standard maintenance plan?

1081. What was the budget or estimated cost for your organizations services?

1082. What was the overall budget or estimated cost?

1083. How is risk transferred?

1084. What was the actual budget or estimated cost for your organizations services?

1085. How does the proposed individual meet each requirement?

1086. What was the final actual cost?

1087. What is the average response time for answering a support call?

1088. What process manages the contracts?

1089. If applicable; describe your standard schedule for new software version releases. Are new software version releases included in the standard maintenance plan?

4.6 Formal Acceptance: Risk Committee

1090. How well did the team follow the methodology?

1091. What is the Acceptance Management Process?

1092. Have all comments been addressed?

1093. What lessons were learned about your Risk Committee project management methodology?

1094. How does your team plan to obtain formal acceptance on your Risk Committee project?

1095. Was the Risk Committee project goal achieved?

1096. Did the Risk Committee project achieve its MOV?

1097. Do you perform formal acceptance or burn-in tests?

1098. Who supplies data?

1099. Was business value realized?

1100. Do you buy pre-configured systems or build your own configuration?

1101. Does it do what Risk Committee project team said it would?

1102. Did the Risk Committee project manager and team act in a professional and ethical manner?

1103. General estimate of the costs and times to complete the Risk Committee project?

1104. What function(s) does it fill or meet?

1105. Was the client satisfied with the Risk Committee project results?

1106. What was done right?

1107. Who would use it?

1108. Was the Risk Committee project managed well?

1109. Is formal acceptance of the Risk Committee project product documented and distributed?

5.0 Closing Process Group: Risk Committee

1110. How critical is the Risk Committee project success to the success of your organization?

1111. What is an Encumbrance?

1112. How well defined and documented were the Risk Committee project management processes you chose to use?

1113. What were the actual outcomes?

1114. Is this a follow-on to a previous Risk Committee project?

1115. What areas does the group agree are the biggest success on the Risk Committee project?

1116. Is there a clear cause and effect between the activity and the lesson learned?

1117. Were the outcomes different from the already stated planned?

1118. Based on your Risk Committee project communication management plan, what worked well?

1119. Will the Risk Committee project deliverable(s) replace a current asset or group of assets?

1120. Did the delivered product meet the specified requirements and goals of the Risk Committee project?

1121. What is the overall risk of the Risk Committee project to your organization?

1122. Can the lesson learned be replicated?

1123. When will the Risk Committee project be done?

1124. Just how important is your work to the overall success of the Risk Committee project?

1125. What were things that you did very well and want to do the same again on the next Risk Committee project?

5.1 Procurement Audit: Risk Committee

1126. Did the contracting authority offer unrestricted and full electronic access to the contract documents and any supplementary documents (specifying the internet address in the notice)?

1127. Is there management monitoring of transactions and balances?

1128. Access to data, including standing data, and the identification of restriction levels and authorised personnel was in place?

1129. Are budget transfers within the general fund made for only the already stated items permitted by law and regulation?

1130. Were results of the award procedures published?

1131. Was the estimation of contract value in accordance with the criteria fixed in the Directive?

1132. What are the required standards of quality assurance or environmental management?

1133. Does the procurement function/unit have the ability to secure best performance from contractors?

1134. Do the buyers always select or authorize the source of supply on other than contract purchases?

1135. Does the strategy ensure that needs are met, and not exceeded?

1136. Is there a record maintained of the procedures followed in the opening of tenders together with the reasons for the acceptance or rejection of tenders received?

1137. Are checks disbursed by someone other than the individual who authorized payment?

1138. Was there a sound basis for the scorings applied to the criteria and was the scoring well balanced?

1139. Was confidentiality ensured when necessary?

1140. Are employees with cash disbursement responsibilities required to take scheduled vacations?

1141. Are advantages and disadvantages of in-house production, outsourcing and Public Private Partnerships considered?

1142. Did your organization permit tenderers to submit variants, thus offering space for creative solutions and added value?

1143. Are approval limits covered in written procedures?

1144. Are behaviour modification applied to change procurement of goods and services if procurement is not functioning properly?

1145. Was invitation to tender to each specific

contract issued after the evaluation of the indicative tenders was completed?

5.2 Contract Close-Out: Risk Committee

1146. Change in knowledge?

1147. Parties: who is involved?

1148. Have all contracts been closed?

1149. Was the contract complete without requiring numerous changes and revisions?

1150. Have all contract records been included in the Risk Committee project archives?

1151. Was the contract sufficiently clear so as not to result in numerous disputes and misunderstandings?

1152. Has each contract been audited to verify acceptance and delivery?

1153. How/when used ?

1154. Have all acceptance criteria been met prior to final payment to contractors?

1155. Have all contracts been completed?

1156. Why Outsource?

1157. What is capture management?

1158. How is the contracting office notified of the

automatic contract close-out?

5.3 Project or Phase Close-Out: Risk Committee

1166. What can you do better next time, and what specific actions can you take to improve?

1167. What security considerations needed to be addressed during the procurement life cycle?

1168. In addition to assessing whether the Risk Committee project was successful, it is equally critical to analyze why it was or was not fully successful. Are you including this?

1169. What was learned?

1170. Did the delivered product meet the specified requirements and goals of the Risk Committee project?

1171. What were the desired outcomes?

1172. Planned completion date?

1173. Were messages directly related to the release strategy or phases of the Risk Committee project?

1174. Who controlled key decisions that were made?

1175. What benefits or impacts does the stakeholder group expect to obtain as a result of the Risk Committee project?

1176. When and how were information needs best met?

1177. Who are the Risk Committee project stakeholders and what are roles and involvement?

1178. If you were the Risk Committee project sponsor, how would you determine which Risk Committee project team(s) and/or individuals deserve recognition?

1179. Complete yes or no?

1180. What was the preferred delivery mechanism?

1181. Does the lesson educate others to improve performance?

1182. What process was planned for managing issues/risks?

5.4 Lessons Learned: Risk Committee

1183. Do you conduct the engineering tests?

1184. How effective was each Risk Committee project Team member in fulfilling his/her role?

1185. Will the information remain current?

1186. Who had fiscal authority to manage the funding for the Risk Committee project, did that work?

1187. What are the internal dependencies?

1188. What Risk Committee project circumstances were not anticipated?

1189. How effective was the training you received in preparation for the use of the product/service?

1190. What are the expectations of the individuals?

1191. Did the Risk Committee project management methodology work?

1192. What were the main sources of frustration in the Risk Committee project?

1193. What specialization does the task require?

1194. How well do you feel the executives supported this Risk Committee project?

1195. What were the key issues?

1196. Were any strategies or activities unsuccessful?

1197. How much of your time was spent on other than this Risk Committee project?

1198. How effectively were issues resolved before escalation was necessary?

1199. How objective was the collection of data?

1200. How effective was Risk Committee project Team member training?

1201. How clearly defined were the objectives for this Risk Committee project?

Index

commitment 96, 112, 128, 181, 225
committed 65, 149, 177, 206
Committee 1-13, 15-42, 44-67, 69-73, 75-126, 128-130, 132,
134-136, 138, 140-146, 149-153, 155, 157-159, 161-173, 175-177,
179, 181, 183-185, 187-195, 197, 199, 201-203, 205-207, 209-217,
219, 222, 224, 226, 228, 230, 232-234, 236, 238-240, 242, 244-248,
251, 253-256
committees 83
common 123, 171, 204
community 134, 165-166, 173, 199
companies 1, 95, 218
company 7, 56, 118
compare 64, 80, 193, 238
compared 112, 205
comparison 10
compatible 215, 234-235
compelling 37
competing 46
complains 226
complaint 226
complaints 194
complete 1, 8, 10, 17, 35, 38, 41, 131, 149, 152-153, 158,
161, 163, 166, 170, 179, 245, 251, 254
completed 11, 29, 31, 34, 122, 151, 175, 191, 223, 250-251
completely 108, 165, 195
completing 106, 145
completion 34-35, 146-147, 157-158, 184, 222, 234, 239, 253
complex 7, 110, 238
complexity 16, 49, 67, 141, 205, 213
compliance 17, 46, 73, 84, 177, 240
compliant 203
components 132, 146, 177, 206
compute 11
computing 108
concept 76
concern 79, 185, 226
concerned 19
concerns 20-21, 117, 230, 242
concise 134
concrete 84, 227, 235
condition 96, 167
conditions 94, 111, 126
conduct 177-178, 204, 255

265

effects 49, 147, 155, 227
efficiency	59, 98
efficient	54, 77, 129, 187, 212
effort	31, 46, 48, 51, 114, 130, 143, 146, 219, 230
efforts	28, 74
Electrical	142
electronic	1, 248
element	237
elements	9, 31, 60, 90, 132, 147, 183, 223, 236-237
Elevator	136
eliminate	199
eliminated	183
embarking	37
embrace	208
emerging	59, 95
employee	81, 105, 228, 242
employees	16, 18-19, 67, 102, 164, 228, 249
employers	125
empower	7
empowered	180
enable 58
enablers	113
encourage	91
engage	113, 189, 226, 229, 234
engagement	56, 125, 193, 230
Engineers	142
enhanced	106
enhancing	93
enough	7, 58, 103, 138, 233
ensure 29, 37, 59, 63, 105, 111-112, 115-116, 134, 177-178, 181,
209, 222, 225, 234-235, 240, 249
ensured	249
ensures	111
ensuring	9, 117, 238
Enterprise	212
entities 51, 130
entity	1, 137
envisaged	129
equally253
equations	163
equipment	25, 163, 225
equipped	33
equitably	41, 224, 234

278

promising 111
promote 51, 70, 240
promptly 172
proper 95, 134
properly 28, 36, 122, 147, 220, 249
property 220
proponents 230
proposals 204, 209
proposed 17, 46, 49, 130, 132, 134, 193, 203, 242
Propriety 232
protect 66, 104
protected 64, 225
protection 108
protocols 224
provide 18, 70, 103, 105, 116, 125, 131, 134, 146, 157, 163, 165, 171, 173, 226, 234, 237
provided 11, 91, 150, 163, 225
providers 79
provides 156
providing 95, 125, 175, 219
provision 202
Public 129, 249
published 248
publisher 1
purchase 7, 163, 203, 223
purchased 147
purchases 248
purpose 2, 9, 124, 161, 174, 187, 217, 227, 233-235
purposes 132, 169
qualified 41, 61, 68-69, 71, 141, 150, 187
qualifies 68, 71
qualify 53, 59, 71
qualities 19, 228
quality 1, 4-5, 9, 24, 47, 50, 53, 59, 68-70, 87, 89, 98, 116, 122, 129, 132-133, 140, 149-150, 163-164, 167, 170, 177, 179-182, 185-186, 188, 201, 206, 209, 214, 217, 219-220, 248
quantified 99
quantify 53
question 10, 15, 27, 43, 58, 74, 89, 101, 114, 129
questions 7-8, 10, 165, 189, 231
quickly 9, 61, 64, 67, 184
quotes 203
radically 58

status   5-6, 70, 135, 140, 147, 149, 169, 183, 188, 194, 201, 211,
230, 236-239, 242
steady 55
steering   143, 188
stored 220
stories 35
strategic   48, 77, 95, 110, 169, 188, 193, 205, 219, 228
strategies   95, 109, 115, 129, 217-218, 220, 256
strategy   15, 38, 44, 74, 85, 94, 104, 112, 117, 132, 190, 203,
217, 249, 253
Stream 60, 62
strengths   132, 155-156
stretch 103
strict   62
strive   103, 210
Strongly   10, 15, 27, 43, 58, 74, 89, 101, 213
structure   3, 50, 75, 110, 141, 144, 161, 168, 207
Structured   105
structures   147, 234, 237
stupid 116
subdivided   183
subject8-9, 32
subjects   71
submit 249
submitted   215
subset 19
sub-teams   226
succeed   52, 156
success   20, 22, 30, 32, 36-37, 41, 45-46, 53, 76-77, 85, 97,
101, 109-111, 114, 116, 140, 158, 171, 192, 196, 211, 217, 234,
246-247
successes   118
successful   63, 90, 107, 117, 128, 161-162, 212, 228, 253
succession   98
sufficient   146, 213
suggest   195
suggested   93, 215
summary   163
supervisor   228
supplier   84, 170, 205
suppliers   34, 59, 72, 107, 187, 220
supplies   244
supply 55, 155, 248

CPSIA information can be obtained
at www.ICGtesting.com
Printed in the USA
BVHW041011200819
556236BV00011B/760/P